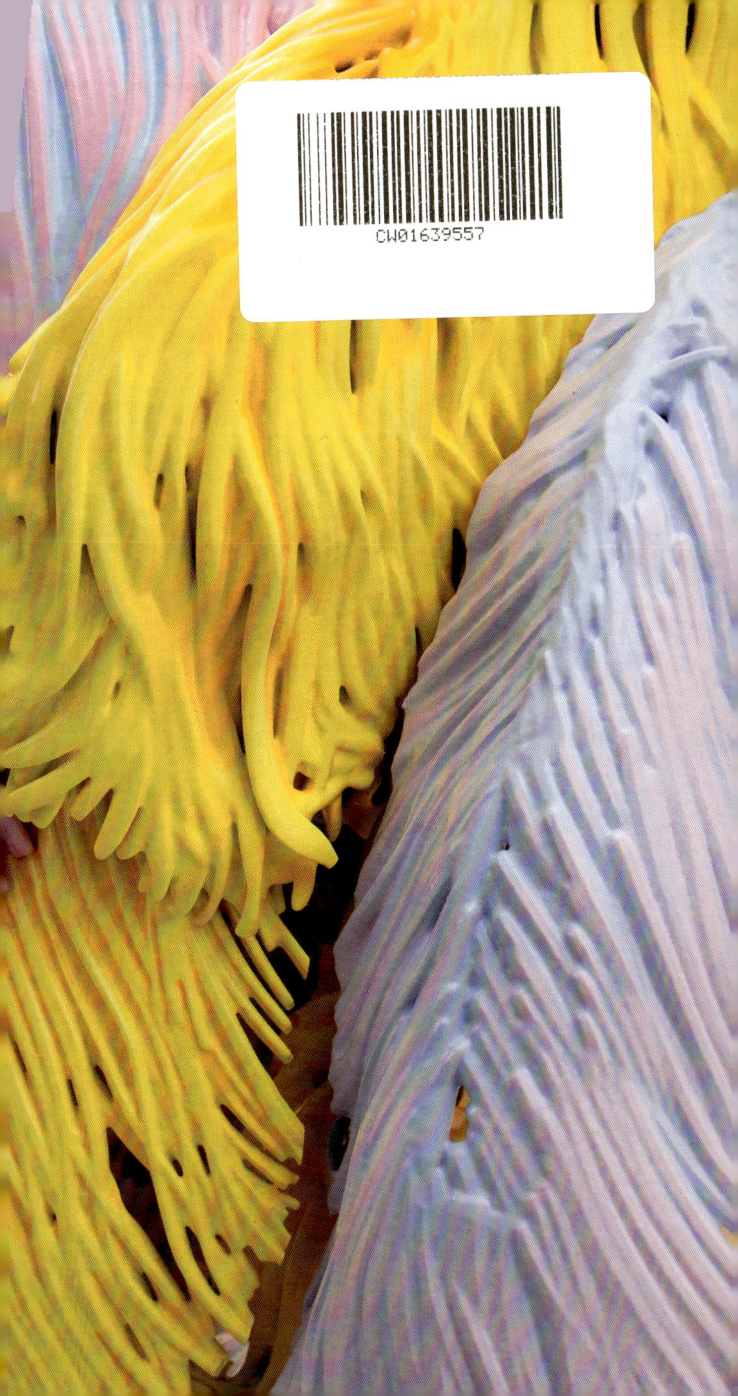

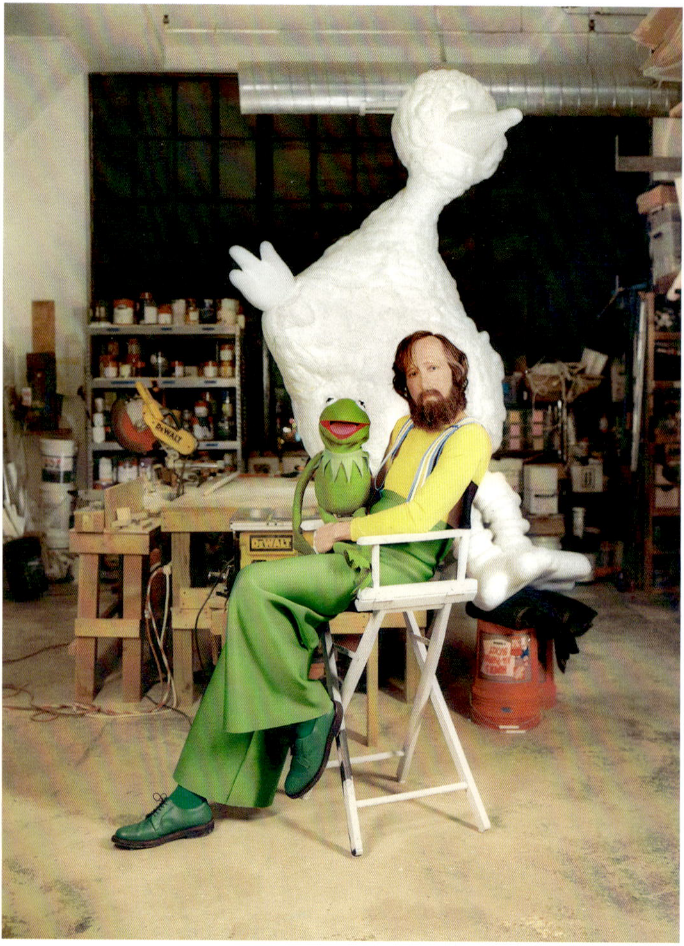
DeWALT
DeWALT

The Roof Garden Commission

Alex Da Corte
As Long as the Sun Lasts

Shanay Jhaveri
Jack Halberstam
Sheena Wagstaff

THE MET
The Metropolitan Museum of Art, New York
Distributed by Yale University Press
New Haven and London

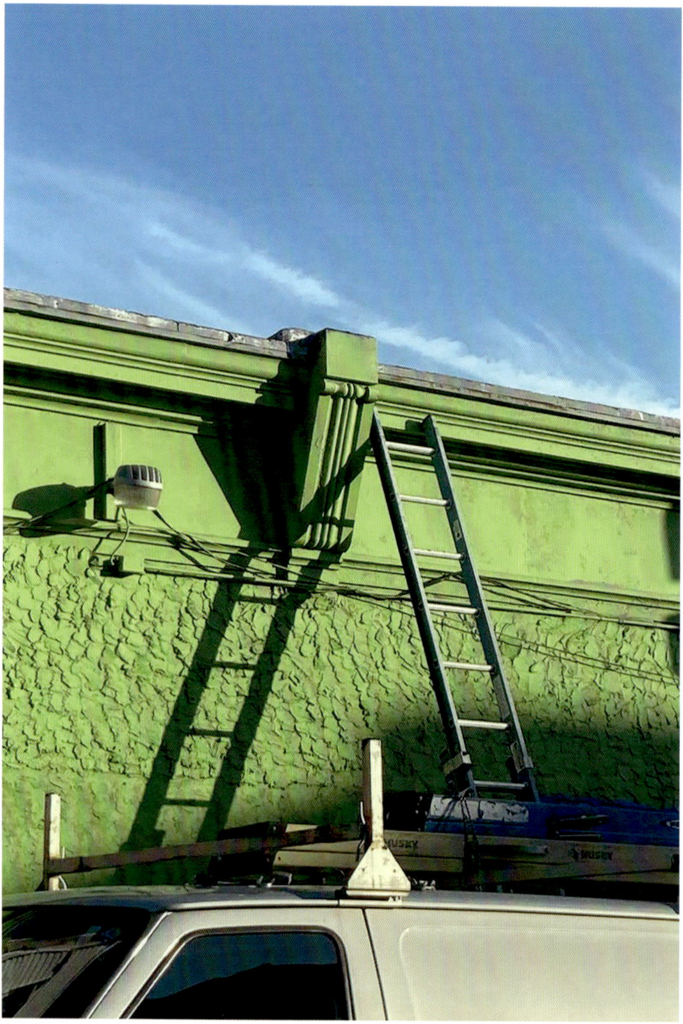

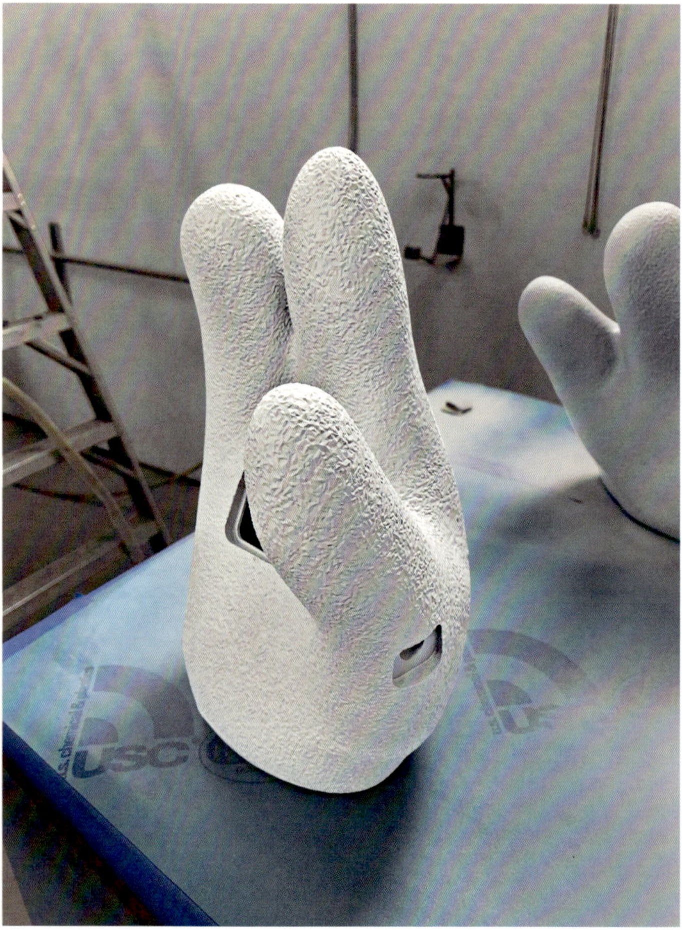
USC

Sponsor's Statement

Bloomberg Philanthropies is proud to partner with The Metropolitan Museum of Art in support of *The Roof Garden Commission: Alex Da Corte, As Long as the Sun Lasts*. For more than a decade, we've sponsored exceptional contemporary art exhibitions on The Iris and B. Gerald Cantor Roof Garden, and Da Corte's contemplative site-specific work continues this tradition. In his monumental kinetic sculpture, the artist brings together *Sesame Street*'s Big Bird and the mobiles of artist Alexander Calder and sets the two cultural icons against New York City's enchanting skyline.

Bloomberg Philanthropies works in 810 cities and 170 countries around the world to ensure better, longer lives for the greatest number of people. The foundation focuses on five key areas for creating lasting change: arts, education, the environment, government innovation, and public health. The arts are a valuable way to engage citizens and strengthen communities. Through innovative partnerships and bold approaches, the Bloomberg Philanthropies Arts program supports increased access to culture through new technologies and empowers artists and cultural organizations to enhance the quality of life in cities.

Bloomberg
Philanthropies

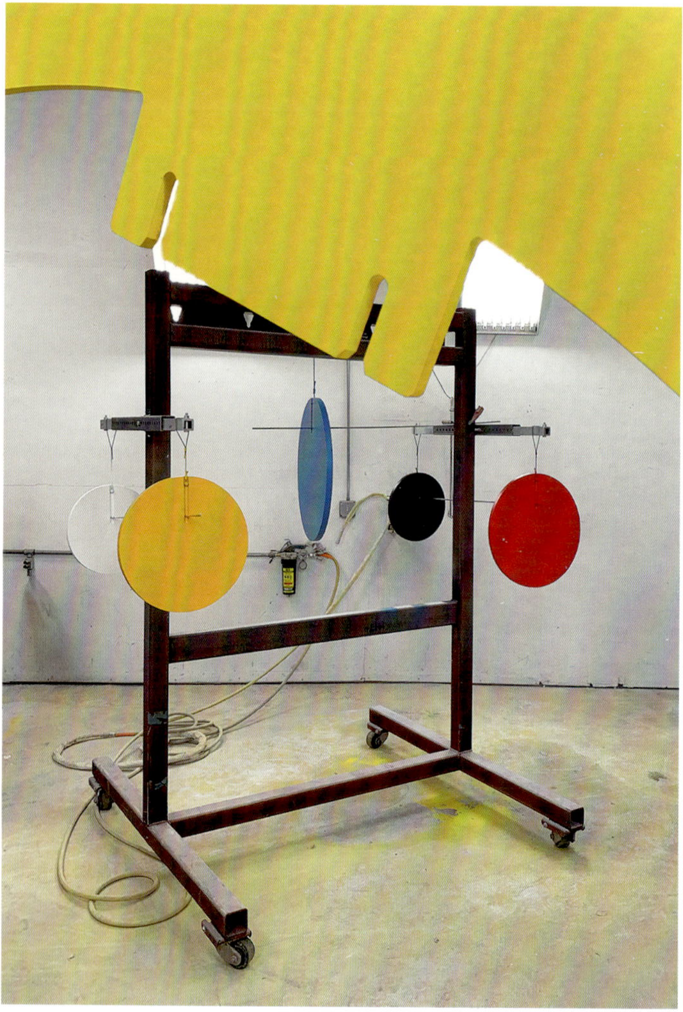

Director's Foreword

With its captivating view of Central Park at the top of The Met, The Iris and B. Gerald Cantor Roof Garden has provided unparalleled inspiration to artists invited to create site-specific artworks for this setting.

This year, we are delighted to present *As Long as the Sun Lasts,* an enchanting commission consisting of a single monumental kinetic sculpture by Alex Da Corte. Known for the cultural icons that inhabit his work, Da Corte has chosen the beloved *Sesame Street* character Big Bird and the sculptural works of Alexander Calder for The Met's commission, which was conceived during the COVID-19 pandemic. For Da Corte, both Big Bird and Calder embody optimism and hope, suggesting that our society can be renewed and reinvigorated despite the challenges of our present moment.

Initiated by Sheena Wagstaff, Leonard A. Lauder Chairman, Department of Modern and Contemporary Art, and organized by Shanay Jhaveri, Assistant Curator, International Modern and Contemporary Art, *As Long as the Sun Lasts* is an inspiring work that joins a distinguished group of annual commissions for this site.

We are grateful to Bloomberg Philanthropies for its enduring support of the Roof Garden Commission series and its important commitment to the Department of Modern and Contemporary Art at large. Cynthia Hazen Polsky and her husband, Leon B. Polsky, are dedicated champions of the Museum, and we thank them for their continued support of this project. Finally, our appreciation goes to the Mary and Louis S. Myers Foundation Endowment Fund for making this publication possible.

Max Hollein
Marina Kellen French Director
The Metropolitan Museum of Art

In Pursuit of a Hopeful Construction

Shanay Jhaveri

On November 16, 1983, PBS aired a one-hour special of the educational children's television series *Sesame Street* called *Don't Eat the Pictures* (fig. 1). Mostly shot on-site at The Metropolitan Museum of Art, the program finds the cast of *Sesame Street* accidentally locked in the Museum after Big Bird goes to find Mr. Snuffleupagus at closing time. Along the way, Big Bird befriends a young Egyptian prince, Sahu, who has been trapped in the galleries, trying to solve the riddle: "Where does today meet yesterday?" Big Bird, while mulling over this quandary, unassumingly answers the riddle: today meets yesterday at a museum like The Met. With Big Bird's help, Sahu is freed, and the episode ends with Big Bird pretending to be a statue in one of the empty niches on the Museum's facade, encouraging viewers to visit their local museum. Thirty-eight years later Big Bird is back at The Met, this time on top of the Museum's roof, as part of *As Long as the Sun Lasts*, a sculpture created by the multidisciplinary artist Alex Da Corte (b. 1980) for The Met's ongoing Roof Garden Commission series.

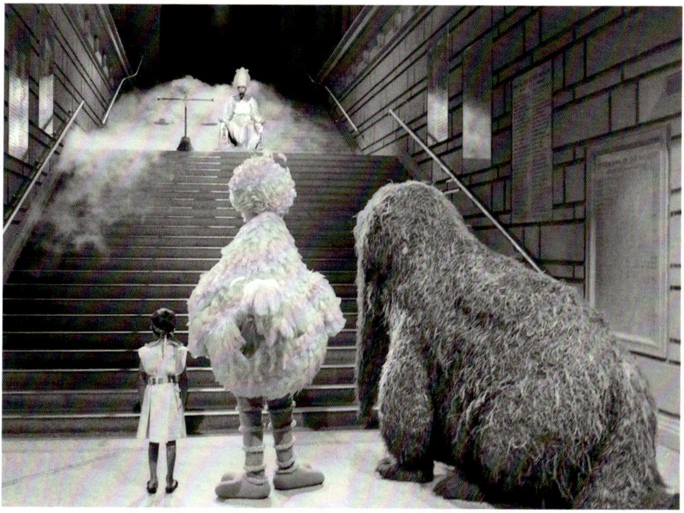

Fig. 1. Still showing Prince Sahu, Big Bird, and Mr. Snuffleupagus in the Great Hall of The Met, from *Don't Eat the Pictures*, 1983, directed by **Jon Stone** (American, 1931–1997)

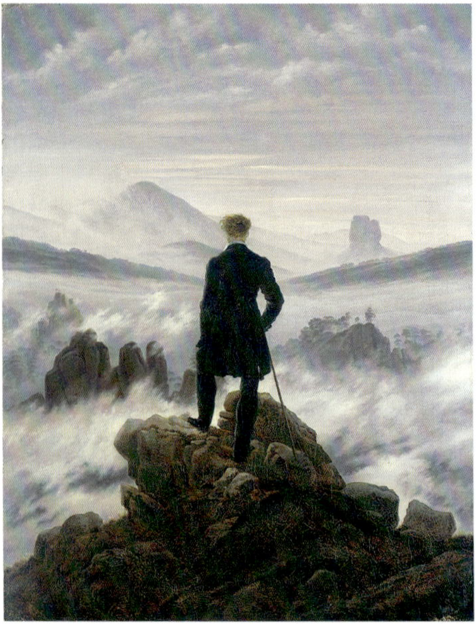

Fig. 2. **Caspar David Friedrich** (German, 1774–1840). *Wanderer above the Sea of Fog*, ca. 1818. Oil on canvas, 37 3/8 × 29 1/2 in. (94.8 × 74.8 cm). Kunsthalle Hamburg, Germany

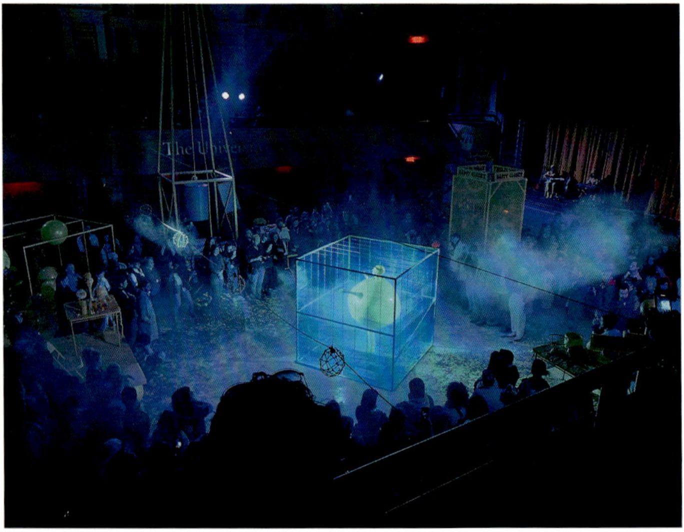

Fig. 3. **Alex Da Corte.** *Chicken*, 2020. Reinvention of Allan Kaprow's *Chicken* at Gershman Hall, University of the Arts, Philadelphia

It is unsurprising that Da Corte would invite Big Bird back to the Museum to be a major player in his project, given that his artistic world is often filled with characters and celebrities from American popular culture. The rapper Eminem, Bugs Bunny, the Wicked Witch from *The Wizard of Oz*, and Mister Rogers, to name a few, have appeared in Da Corte's moving-image works, such as *TRUƎ LIFƎ* (2013, see fig. 22) and *Rubber Pencil Devil* (2018, see figs. 16–18, 28). His practice has also involved the quoting, reimagining, or inclusion of works by established artists. Take, for example, his installation *Die Hexe* (2015, fig. 4), in which he integrated artworks by Mike Kelley, Bjarne Melgaard, Robert Gober, and Haim Steinbach; the repositioning of a Christopher Wool painting on its side in *Le Miroir Vivant* (2015); or the wholesale reinvention of a work, as in the case of Allan Kaprow's 1962 happening *Chicken* (fig. 3), which Da Corte staged in 2020. In his sculpture for

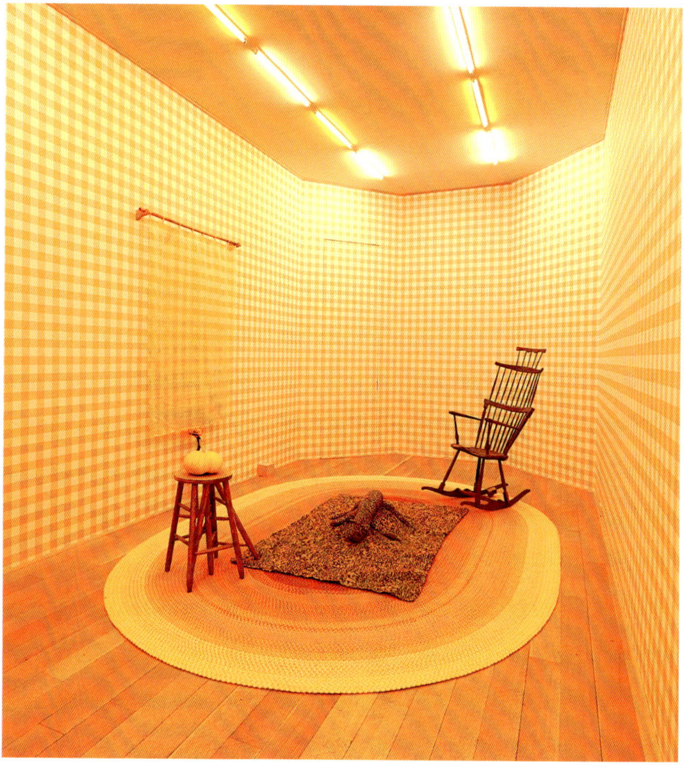

Fig. 4. **Alex Da Corte.** *Die Hexe*, 2015. Installation view, Luxembourg & Dayan, New York

The Met's Iris and B. Gerald Cantor Roof Garden, Da Corte "introduces" Big Bird, who is nested on a mobile-like sculptural form, to the world of artist Alexander Calder.

Da Corte has always excelled in devising tableaux or scenarios in which appropriated figures, artworks, and certain objects of mass culture are made to commingle and coexist. These past orchestrations share carefully constructed setups, such as Technicolor backgrounds, neon-light frames, wallpaper, or extensive artificial materials, that transform them into immersive environments. For *As Long as the Sun Lasts* Da Corte contends with Central Park, the New York skyline, and the sky itself as his backdrop. These are not components he can, or wishes to, manage. Instead, he sees the installation as being in the "hands" of the sky, and so he brings to the roof of The Met only a gently rotating large-scale sculpture. It could strike someone as absurd to draw together Calder's hybrid standing mobiles and Big Bird from *Sesame Street* in a single sculpture and orient them toward the New York skyline, but these elements coalesce in this setting.

Big Bird, an eight-foot-two-inch anthropomorphic yellow bird who has graced the cover of *Time* magazine, is the symbol of *Sesame Street*. An embodiment of youthful curiosity and kindness, but equally shy and prone to puzzlement and bewilderment, Big Bird is a gentle, endearing surrogate through whom children can grapple with the complexities of navigating society and its attendant injustices and cruelties. *Sesame Street* was born of the progressive federal policies of the 1960s and the earnest ambitions of educators; in 2015, the show's first-run programming began premiering on HBO, and it continues to air for free on PBS KIDS, an action that has occasioned much discussion.[1]

Decades before the debut of *Sesame Street*, the artist Alexander Calder began constructing ingenious kinetic abstract compositions that brought motion and mobility to the formal language of modernism. In his recent biography, Jed Perl noted that "Calder's classicism grew out of his most basic feelings as a person who both early and late, as a child and as a man, knew how to play."[2] Without a doubt, this "classical seriousness," to quote Perl, is inherent to Calder's works of the 1930s and 1940s, some of which initially were motorized, and then were meant to move with the natural changes in the environment in which they were installed. Perhaps Calder's greater contribution to modern art is the perceptual challenge these moving works offer in their light, fluid dynamism. For viewers there is no fixed place or position from which to grasp them. They evade monumentality, and involve the viewer in an exchange of infinite possibilities. Simple, immediately likable, easily reproducible, they slid into the world of sleek commercial design over the second half of the last century.

The familiarity and recognizability of Calder's sculptures and the characters of *Sesame Street* have made them enduringly accessible to Da Corte. As he discusses in his interview with Sheena Wagstaff (see p. 36), he is committed to finding new ways of looking at things we find familiar: a preexisting connection or relation becomes the pathway to fantasizing, to jump-starting his imagination. His creative process involves appropriating cultural icons and activating them through subtle transformations, because he does not "think of sculpture as static, as dead objects. I think of them as tracing an action. Sculpture is the unravelling of a familiar object."[3] In a review of Da Corte's work, the writer Annie Godfrey Larmon noted that he brings his own personal associations to these icons and a subjective logic by "attending to the ways in which objects persist in the material world—inviting our tactile response and persistently collecting traces of how they have been touched and where they have been."[4]

Da Corte began to gather his thoughts for the Roof Garden Commission during the height of the COVID-19 pandemic in 2020—a dispiriting, difficult, and deadly time. In self-isolation in Philadelphia, Da Corte found himself having to contend with his own loneliness, anxiety, and fear, as well as a pervasive sense of uncertainty, not only regarding when the pandemic and the restrictions it brought to collective life would end but also their implications for the future, one that already felt diminished and denuded. Searching for comfort and reassurance, Da Corte gravitated to Big Bird and Calder's standing mobiles for what they have been known to represent. Could these popular icons sit with him and help him take a long, hard look into an unknown tomorrow? Accordingly, he set out modeling and sketching, and the two have now come to the Museum's roof.

Da Corte's sculpture has a base of three interlocking pieces and a top in which a shaft with a crescent moon sits on one end and five spheres on the other. In its simplicity, efficient construction, and ease of assembly and disassembly, the sculpture has clear affinities with Calder's standing mobiles. Da Corte is particularly drawn to Calder's *Gallows and Lollipops* (1960), a large-scale outdoor sculpture installed at Da Corte's alma mater Yale University, which may be the primary model for *As Long as the Sun Lasts*. At nearly twenty feet tall, Da Corte's sculpture also shares the imposing scale of many of Calder's later standing mobiles. However, Da Corte crafted the interlocking pieces of his sculpture to resemble Little Tikes Activity Gym outdoor play sets (fig. 5), which debuted in 1987 and could be constructed without the use of standard hardware. Da Corte was especially attracted to the functionality of the Little Tikes modular plastic forms, which can be constantly reconfigured. He cut into a smaller version of the

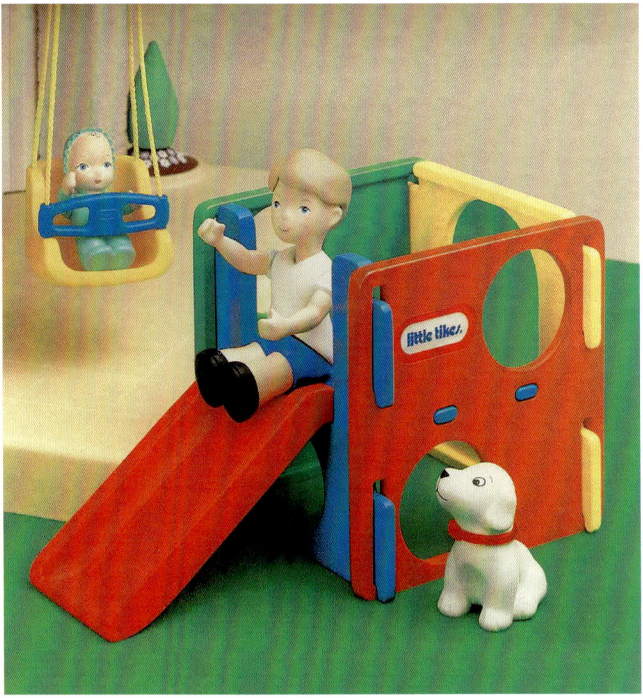

Fig. 5. Promotional ad for Little Tikes Activity Gym, 1989

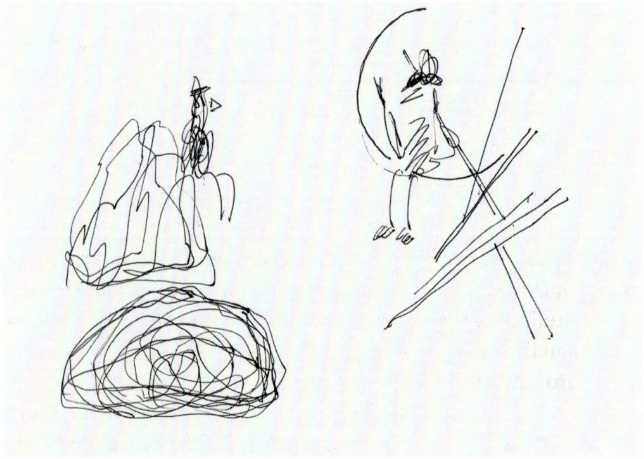

Fig. 6. **Alex Da Corte.** Studies for *As Long as the Sun Lasts*, 2021; studio image from 2020

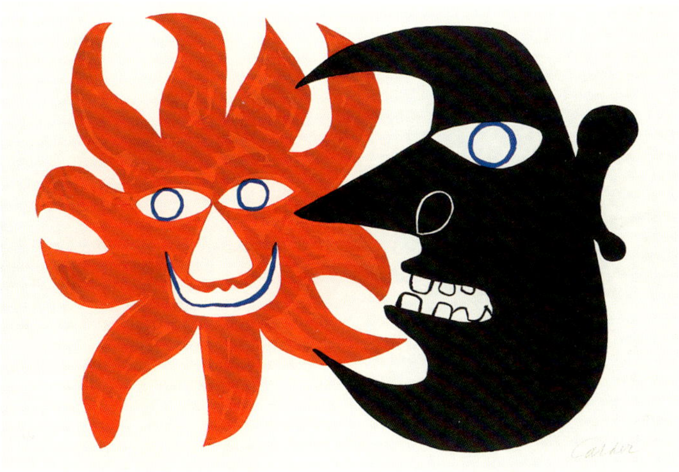

Fig. 7. **Alexander Calder** (American, 1898–1976). *Deux Têtes,* 1975. Lithograph, 23 × 40 in. (58.5 × 101.5 cm)

Little Tikes play set from 1989 to arrive at the shape of his base, which was then enlarged to become the three pieces of the sculpture. By fashioning his sculpture in the modular language of children's outdoor play sets, Da Corte evokes the liveliness and unpredictability of Calder's practice, and employs Calder's use of simple materials to engender the possibility of building new worlds.

Da Corte's standing mobile also reflects Calder's abiding interest in nature's dynamic magnitudes (fig. 7), which crystallized in 1922 after Calder experienced the sun and the moon in the sky at the same time during a sea voyage off the coast of Guatemala. Calder later reflected on his work: "When I have used spheres and discs, I have intended that they should represent more than what they just are. More or less as the earth is a sphere, but also has some miles of gas about it, volcanoes upon it, and the moon making circles around it, and as the sun is a sphere—but also is a source of intense heat, the effect of which is felt at great distances."[5] Enamored of this creative act of translation, Da Corte approximated these ideas for his own standing mobile by including a large crescent moon on one side and five planetary spheres on the other.

Into this micro-universe fashioned from Calder's aesthetic tool kit, Da Corte has inserted Big Bird, who sits on the crescent moon (fig. 6), a ladder in hand, gazing at the sky. However, Da Corte did not render Big Bird in the trademark canary-yellow hue but in

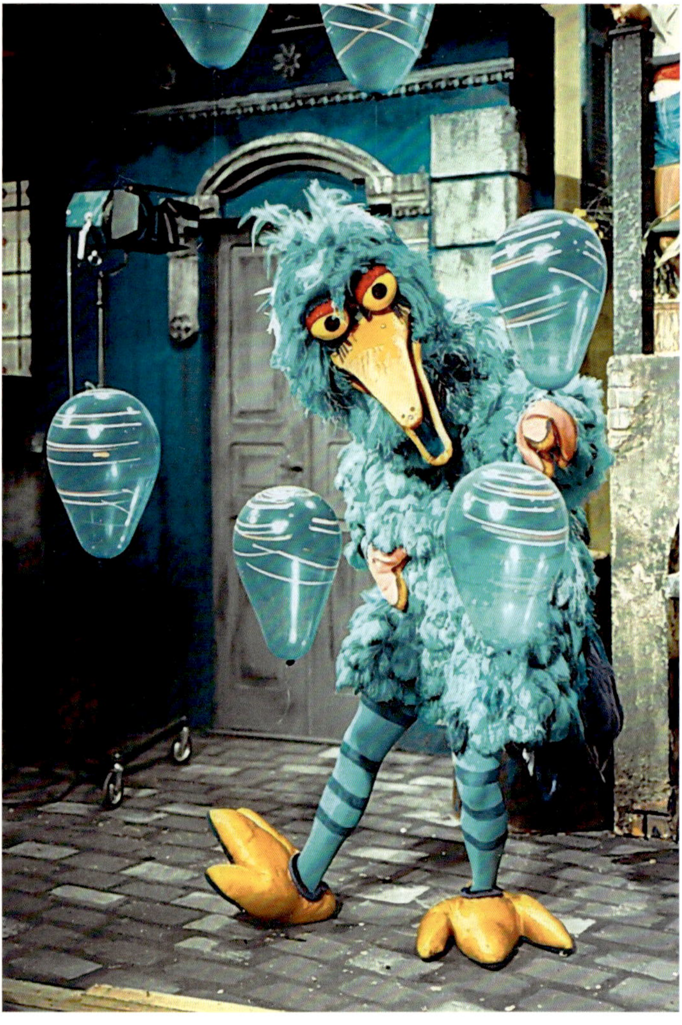

Fig. 8. Garibaldo on the set of *Vila Sésamo* (1972–77)

blue, a color often associated with a state of melancholia. Da Corte's motivation for this change is not arbitrary or wholly subjective but is instead informed and guided by references from the larger *Sesame Street* universe. The artist spent a number of his formative years in Caracas, Venezuela, where as a child he would watch *Vila Sésamo*, the Brazilian coproduction of *Sesame Street*, in which the resident counterpart to Big Bird was Garibaldo (fig. 8), who was blue. Furthermore, in the 1985 film *Sesame Street Presents: Follow That Bird*, Big Bird is captured on a road trip by two carnival operators, painted blue, and forced to perform the song "I'm So Blue" during an act called *The Bluebird of Happiness* (fig. 10).

Da Corte's Big Bird is an amalgam of personal associations, a mix of both Garibaldo and the version of the character from *The Bluebird of Happiness*, a memory from his childhood but also a trapped being. In *As Long as the Sun Lasts*, Big Bird has been liberated from a cage and is no longer forced to perform. The character is now alone, settled on a moon, in a state of contemplation, suspended somewhere between the earth and the larger universe that lies beyond. This hiatus offers Big Bird a moment of repose and allows the character to remain outside of the realm of action and decision. Hannah Arendt has posited that philosophers must remove themselves from the world to think, because "thinking is 'out of order' not merely because it stops all the other activities so necessary for the business of living and staying alive, but because it inverts all ordinary relationships: what is near and appears directly to our senses is now far away and what is distant is actually present."[6] The necessity of physically being at a remove, of having to leave to contemplate, is crucial.

When mining The Met's collection for artistic references, Da Corte saw an inflection of his blue Big Bird in the seven works known as the Unicorn Tapestries (1495–1505, fig. 9), which depict scenes of a hunt of the magical creature. Da Corte was most drawn to the tapestry *The Unicorn Rests in a Garden*, in which the unicorn is tethered to a tree and constrained by a fence. However, the chain is not secured and the fence is low enough for the unicorn to scale, meaning it could escape, but instead it decides to stay in place. Da Corte envisions that his blue Big Bird will have to face a similar decision. Removed from earth, the character holds on to a ladder: is this a means of escape from a collapsed planet, a way to continue exploring elsewhere, or an affirmation to return to earth? Does Big Bird want to leave this world behind?

Potential clues might be found in Da Corte's other artistic inspirations, which range from the solitary figure in Caspar David Friedrich's painting *Wanderer above the Sea of Fog* (ca. 1818, fig. 2) to

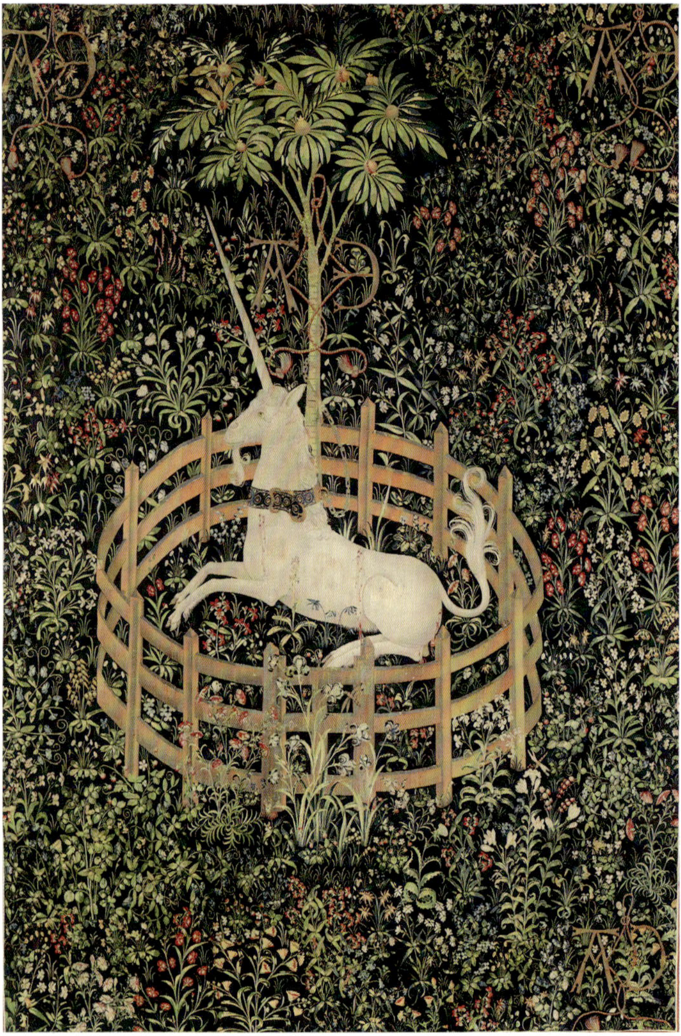

Fig. 9. *The Unicorn Rests in a Garden,* from the Unicorn Tapestries, 1495–1505. Wool, silk and metal threads, 144 7⁄8 × 99 in. (368 × 251.5 cm). The Metropolitan Museum of Art, New York, Gift of John D. Rockefeller Jr., 1937 (37.80.6)

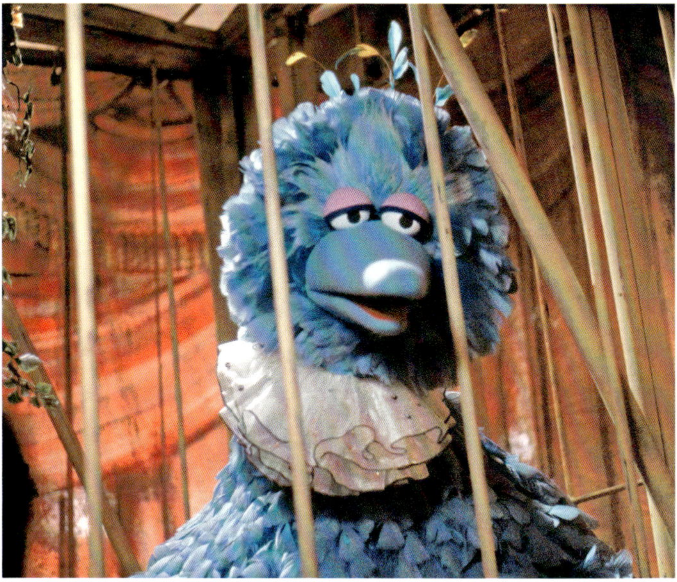

Fig. 10. Still from *Sesame Street Presents: Follow That Bird,* 1985, directed by **Ken Kwapis** (American, born 1957)

the music of Donna Summer to the short-story collection *Cosmicomics* by Italo Calvino, from which Da Corte also drew the name of the commission, *As Long as the Sun Lasts*. Friedrich's work portrays a romantic archetype standing at a precipice, contemplating his place in the world and an unknown future. In contrast, Donna Summer is coolly draped on a crescent moon on the cover of her 1976 *Four Seasons of Love* album (fig. 12). Recounting a love story through the seasons, she is sure that despite the heartbreak of a failed romance, love will come again. Or could Big Bird feel similarly to the lovers set adrift from earth in Italo Calvino's existential story "The Distance of the Moon," from *Cosmicomics,* who muse: "I should have been happy: as I had dreamed, I was alone with her, that intimacy of the Moon. . . . I thought only of the Earth. It was the Earth that caused each of us to be that someone he was rather than someone else."[7]

Then again, the use of this ladder might be an improbability: Da Corte modeled it on the so-called immovable ladder under the window of the Church of the Holy Sepulchre in Jerusalem (fig. 11), which has remained in its place since the 1750s. Because governance of the building is shared by six of the oldest Christian churches, no one group can take possession of the ladder, and it remains in place.

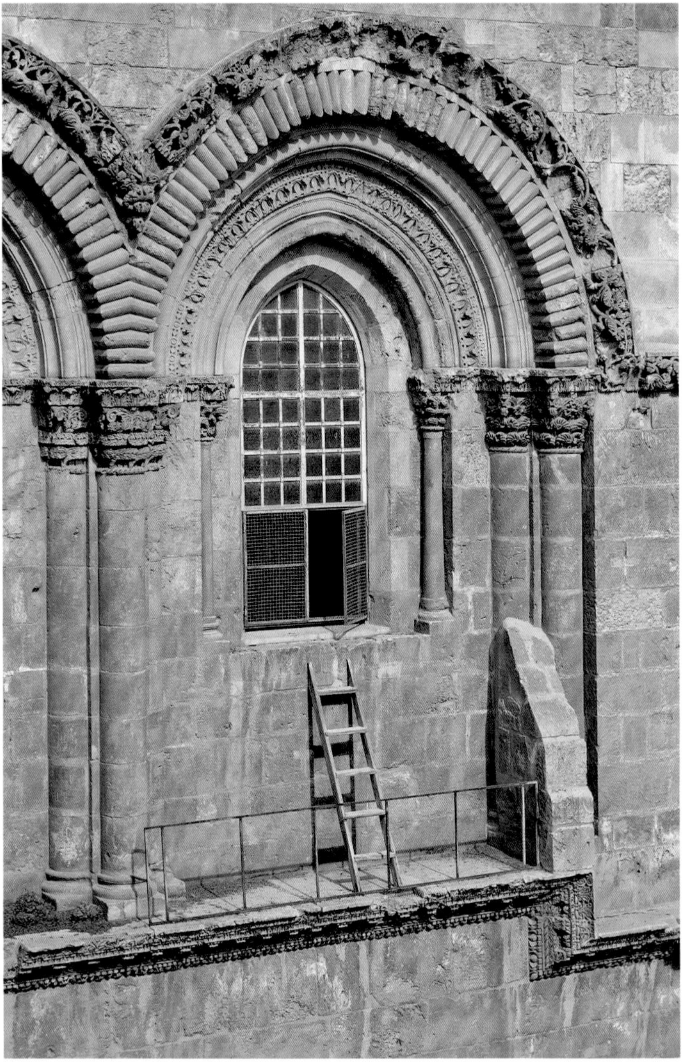

Fig. 11. The so-called immovable ladder of the Church of the Holy Sepulchre in Jerusalem, which has remained in place since the 1750s

Da Corte's Big Bird appears to be mulling over the current state of the world. Is society at the brink, or has it already gone to pieces, signaling that there is no earth to return to—an alternative considered in the essay by Jack Halberstam (see p. 26)? For the purposes of this discussion, let us imagine that there is the possibility of regeneration on earth. Perhaps it is precisely our devolving world, with a surging pandemic, the rise of fascist politics, growing social and racial inequality, and the acceleration of climate change, that provides Big Bird with the ultimate motivation to return. These urgent challenges spark a renewal of faith that this earth can and needs to be fostered, furthered, and cultivated. Despite knowing these issues will never be entirely addressed, and that certainly there will always be another set of calamities to contend with, Da Corte—through his representation of Calder's work and use of Big Bird's persona—appears to meet our current realities with at least the promise of optimism.

At the same time, this revelation of a different world cannot be willed into happening; it requires commitment, collective solidarity, and empathy. Indeed, Da Corte proposes that a sense of a shared communal responsibility is crucial to reanimating the world, musing that the armored construction of Big Bird is composed of a "community" of roughly 7,000 individually placed laser-cut aluminum feathers "acting together to form Big Bird's skin/shell."[8] But Da Corte also suggests that actions of togetherness demand even the briefest moment of being "blue," because as James Baldwin has stated, "the acceptance of this anguish one finds in the blues, and the expression of it, creates also, however odd this may sound, a kind of joy. Now joy is a true state, it is a reality; it has nothing to do with what most people have in mind when they talk of happiness, which is not a real state and does not really exist."[9]

As Long as the Sun Lasts calls for us to pause, to reflect, even to mourn, but ultimately it is a statement of belief in the potential of transformation. The Museum's roof as a site for this sculpture seems an apposite exemplification of this revelation: it is a manifestation of "where today meets yesterday," as Big Bird surmised back in 1983. But, like the ever-changing realities of contemporary life, the sculpture and the viewer's perception of it intermittently shift. Advances are made, but they transpire in fits and starts. There is a continuing labor that is involved, whether it is invisible labor like the wind making the sculpture move, or that of a puppeteer like Caroll Spinney, who played Big Bird throughout his lifetime.

As Rebecca Solnit has eloquently summarized, "The paradises built in hell are improvisational; we make them up as we go along, and in doing so they call on all our strength and creativity and leave us

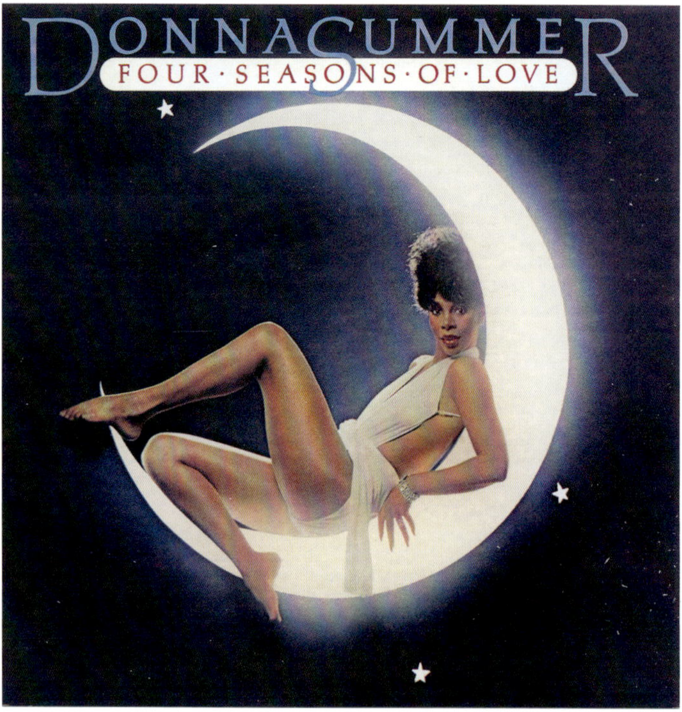

Fig. 12. **Donna Summer** (American, 1948–2012) on the cover of her album *Four Seasons of Love*, 1976

free to invent even as we find ourselves enmeshed in community. These paradises built in hell show us both what we want and what we can be."[10] It is this pursuit of a hopeful construction that motivated Calder and that Da Corte imagines will tempt Big Bird back to earth to be the unicorn or the wanderer, searching out another tomorrow until the sun sets, all the while listening to Donna Summer croon:

> Spring affair, spring affair, spring affair
> And I'm hung up on you
> Spring affair, spring affair, spring affair
> And we got something new, oh yeah, me and you, oh baby[11]

Notes

1. Emily Steel, "'Sesame Street' to Air First on HBO for Next 5 Seasons," *New York Times*, August 13, 2015, www.nytimes.com/2015/08/14/business/media/sesame-street-heading-to-hbo-in-fall.html.
2. Jed Perl, "The Classical Style," in *Calder: The Conquest of Time; The Early Years, 1898–1940* (New York: Alfred A. Knopf, 2017), p. 600.
3. Grela Orihuela and Bill Bilowit, "Moving Image: Alex Da Corte's TRUE LIFE," *Whitewall Art*, April 15, 2013, www.whitewall.art/art/moving-image-alex-da-cortes-true-life.
4. Annie Godfrey Larmon, "Openings: Alex Da Corte," *Artforum*, Summer 2015, www.artforum.com/print/201506/openings-alex-da-corte-52283.
5. Alexander Calder, "What Abstract Art Means to Me," *Museum of Modern Art Bulletin* 18, no. 3 (Spring 1951), pp. 8–9.
6. Hannah Arendt, *The Life of the Mind*, vol. 1, *Thinking* (New York: Harcourt Brace Jovanovich, 1981), p. 85.
7. Italo Calvino, "The Distance of the Moon," in *The Complete Cosmicomics*, trans. Martin McLaughlin, Tim Parks, and William Weaver (London: Penguin Classics, 2009), p. 15.
8. Alex Da Corte, correspondence with the author, December 5, 2020.
9. James Baldwin, "The Uses of the Blues," in *The Cross of Redemption: Uncollected Writings*, ed. Randall Kenan (New York: Vintage Books, 2011), p. 70.
10. Rebecca Solnit, "Epilogue: The Doorway in the Ruins," in *A Paradise Built in Hell: The Extraordinary Communities That Arise in Disaster* (New York: Penguin Books, 2009), p. 312.
11. Donna Summer, vocalist, "Spring Affair," written by Pete Bellotte, Giorgio Moroder, and Donna Summer, track 1 on *Four Seasons of Love*, released October 11, 1976.

Stairway to Heaven

Jack Halberstam

The mobile is a hanging sculpture that marries air to motion, promises balance and harmony, and offers proof of the kinetic hum of life. Like a weather vane, a compass, a scale, or a divining rod, it reminds humans that the world around us speaks constantly in languages and sounds that escape our ears. But in Alex Da Corte's sculptural masterpiece *As Long as the Sun Lasts,* the spectacle of a *Sesame Street* Muppet on the moon bumps humans out of the picture altogether and simultaneously shatters the clichéd arrangements of lunar attractions, aesthetic mastery, masculine will, and feminine submission that are so central to the mythology of the moon. Big Bird—an androgynous, yellow, loud figure of fun—represents not just the infantilization of aesthetics in general but also the scrambling of time, space, art, bodies, and puppetry. In *As Long as the Sun Lasts,* Big Bird has been painted blue as if to indicate a change of mood, a lurking melancholia, and a transition from day to night. With Da Corte's Big (blue) Bird of unfreedom sitting precariously on a sliver of the moon, the artist's anti-monument announces the end of man, the end of world, the end of endings. As if to compensate for that precarity, Big Bird gives the viewer a ladder to nowhere and all the utopian energy that nowhere implies. What, I will ask, can the *Sesame Street* Muppet offer by way of consolation for total collapse?

In the extraordinary painting *Ladder to the Moon* from 1958 (fig. 13), Georgia O'Keeffe also suspended a ladder between earth and moon. The moon, a neatly sliced half, is tiny, lost in the vast expanse of crepuscular turquoise, and it seems barely bright enough to throw the mountains below into dark relief. The painting takes the elements of a desert landscape and rearranges the scale of their relation such that human endeavor and celestial light alike are lost within the vast sky. They are swallowed whole and separated in a way that suggests not just impending darkness or impossible travel but total separation.

The idea of a ladder to the moon has offered itself to a range of artists besides O'Keeffe, such as Joan Miró, with his sculpture *Moonbird* (1946, fig. 14); Italo Calvino, as embodied in his short story "The Distance of the Moon," about frustration and longing; and Alexander Calder, as evidenced in his abstract sculpture

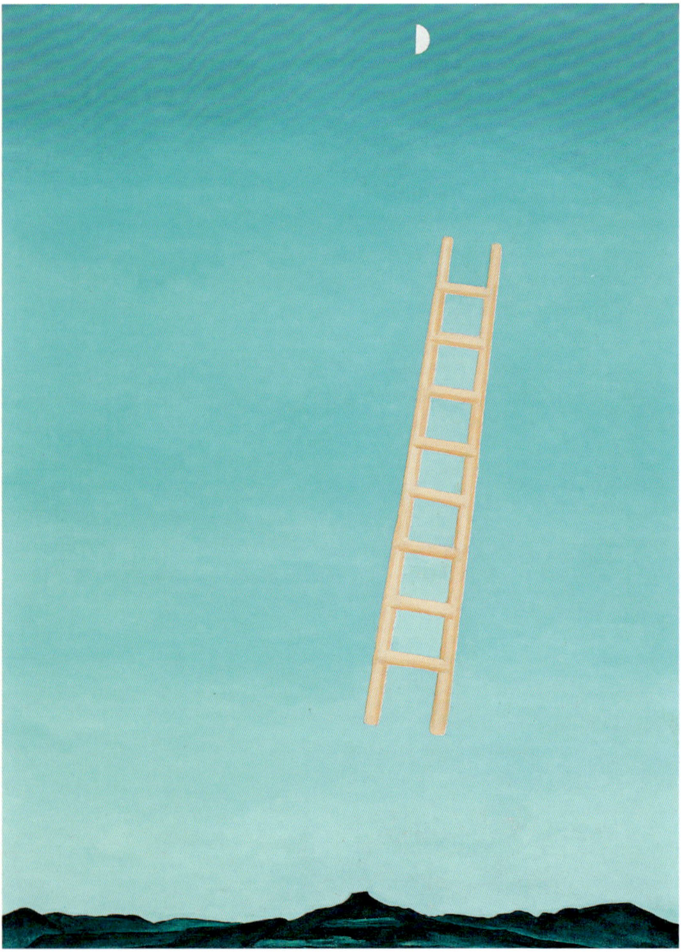

Fig. 13. **Georgia O'Keeffe** (American, 1887–1986). *Ladder to the Moon*, 1958. Oil on canvas, 40 3⁄16 × 30 1⁄4 × 1 3⁄8 in. (102.1 × 76.8 × 3.5 cm). Whitney Museum of American Art, New York; Promised gift of Emily Fisher Landau (P.2010.216a-b)

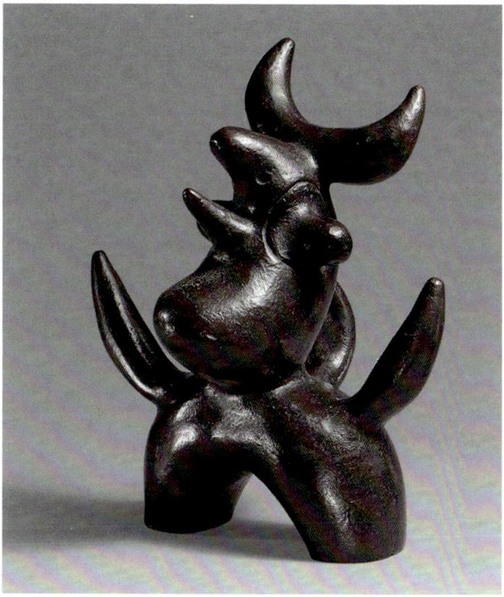

Fig. 14. **Joan Miró** (Spanish, 1893–1983). *Moonbird*, 1946. Bronze, 7 1/4 × 6 1/2 × 4 1/2 in. (18.4 × 16.5 × 11.4 cm). The Metropolitan Museum of Art, New York, The Pierre and Maria-Gaetana Matisse Collection, 2002 (2002.456.121)

Fig. 15. **Alexander Calder** (American, 1898–1976). *Two Moons*, 1969. Sheet metal, wire, and paint, 30 × 48 × 18 in. (76.2 × 121.9 × 45.7 cm)

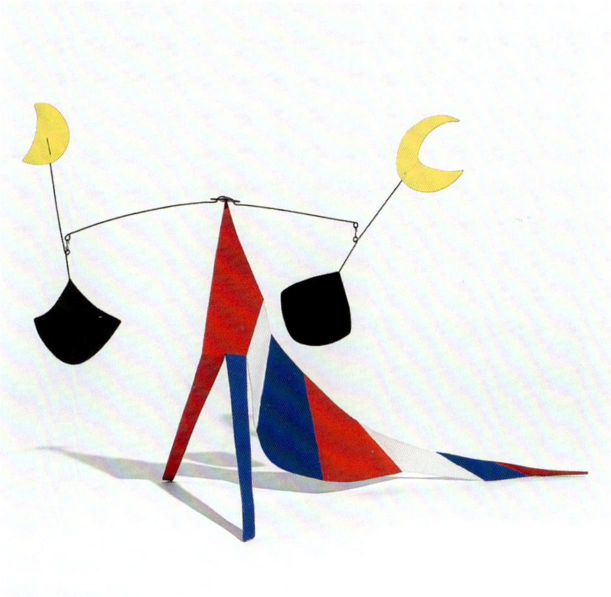

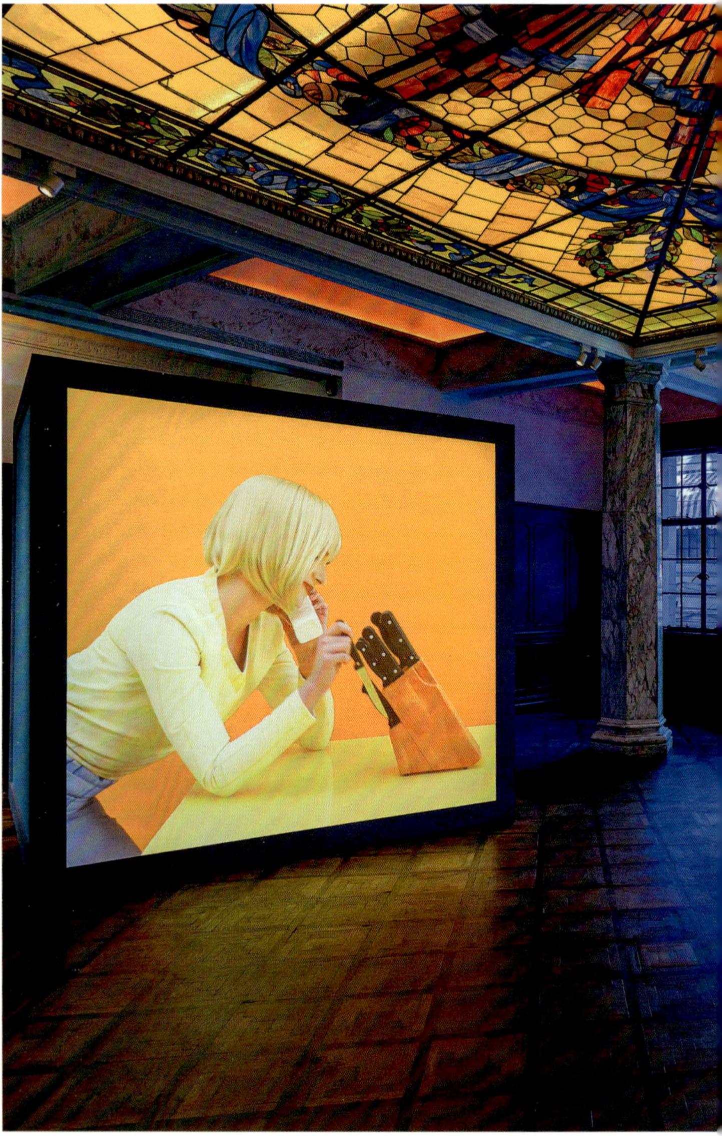

Fig. 16. **Alex Da Corte.** *Rubber Pencil Devil*, 2018. Installation view, Prada Rong Zhai, Shanghai, 2020

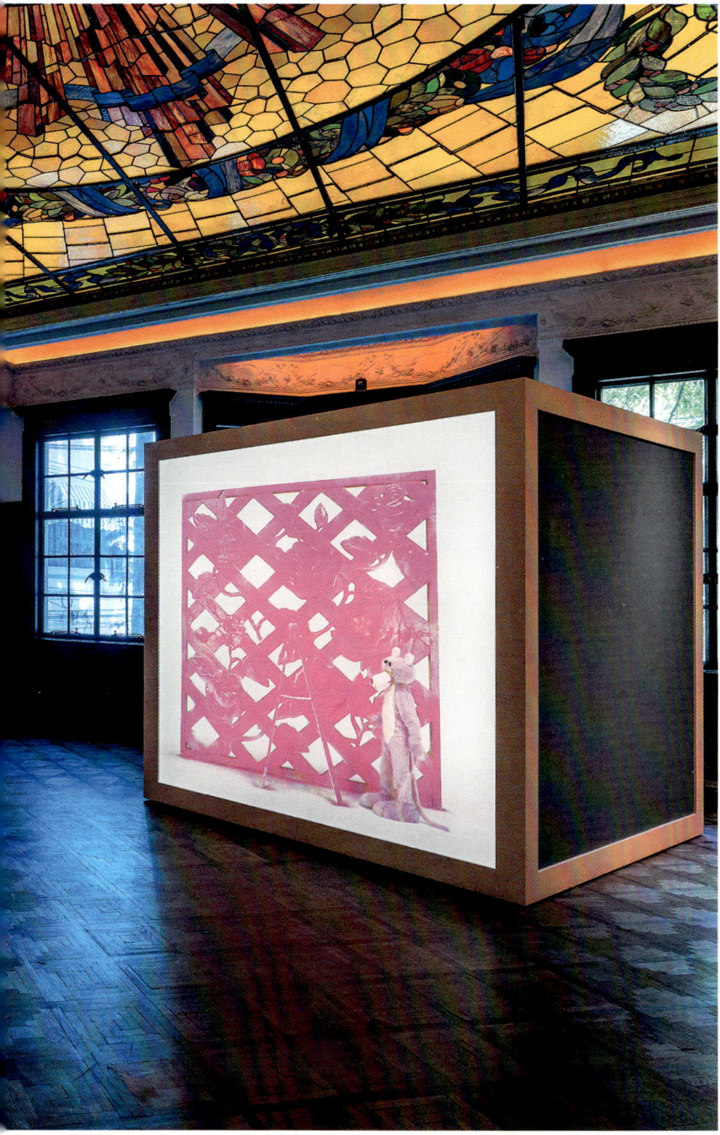

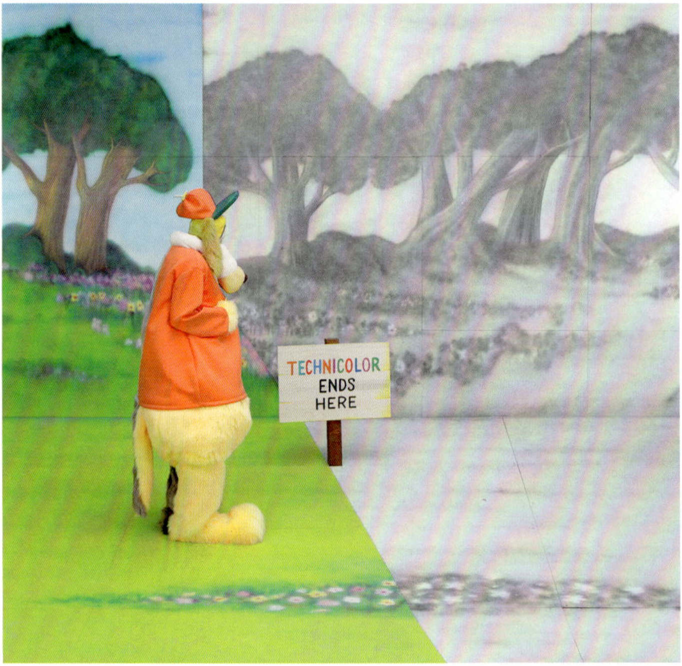

Fig. 17. **Alex Da Corte.** *Rubber Pencil Devil,* 2018. Video, color, sound, 159 min., 22 sec.

Two Moons (1969, fig. 15), titled after the fact of creation. But the fantasy of climbing to the moon or flying there like a bird is replete with treacherous clichés—in Calvino's overwrought story, for example, the moon is made of cheese and squirts milk, and men catapult themselves there in order to experience the pleasures and products of its maternal body. To circumvent the clichés, O'Keeffe abstracts the moon, offering an image of it not as an orb but as a small hole, a tear really, in the fabric of the sky. As for Calder, his abstract work captures the dynamism of nature's forces.

Alex Da Corte's installation work revels in the absurdity of the object. He plays with scale, as in *Rubber Pencil Devil* (2018, figs. 16, 17), in which animated beings move through neon-hued TV sets and elves dance and engage in fetishistic behavior. Da Corte also experiments with televisual environments, exploring the differences between color and black and white, between goofiness and melancholia, between puppets, cartoons, and humans. By highlighting introspection, abstraction, and perversion, Da Corte rejects the stark division between children's

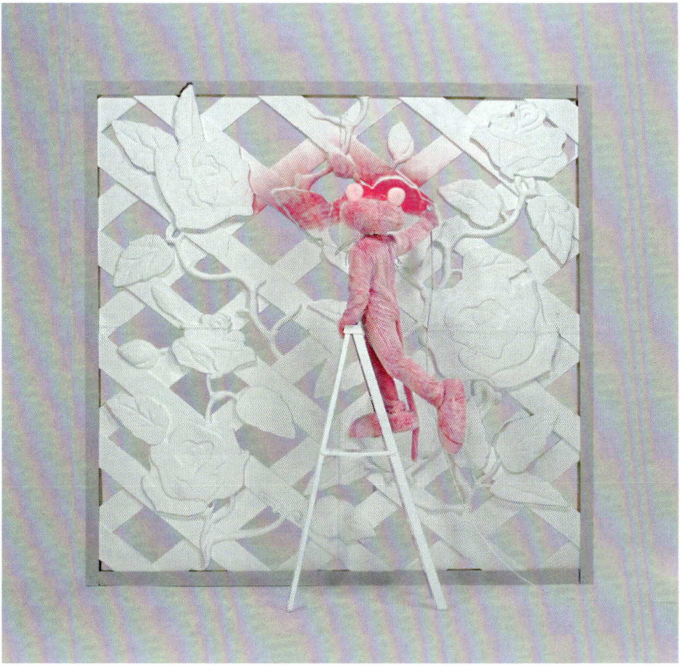

Fig. 18. **Alex Da Corte.** *Rubber Pencil Devil,* 2018. Video, color, sound, 159 min., 22 sec.

fantasy worlds and the supposedly complex internal landscapes of adulthood, fusing high and low, the abstract and the figurative, in seductive arrangements of bodies and space. Da Corte's work smashes the representational regimes of high modernism but then pulls forms and color schemes, lines and background noise out of the wreckage to be used anew. In one segment in *Rubber Pencil Devil* (fig. 18), Da Corte transforms into his version of the cartoon character the Pink Panther, who paints a large-scale surface pink and then becomes nothing but a disappearing pink line. In so doing, the artist offers simultaneous commentary on the color pink, the disappearance of the figure/ground distinction, and the foregrounding of fantasy (the animated character of the Pink Panther) over performance (Peter Sellers as Inspector Clouseau in the film *The Pink Panther*). Ultimately, Da Corte invests in the bubbly, oversaturated imagery of popular culture while infusing it with aesthetic seriousness and gravity.

Gravity is also at issue in Da Corte's rooftop sculpture for The Met (fig. 19). *As Long as the Sun Lasts* bundles metaphors and

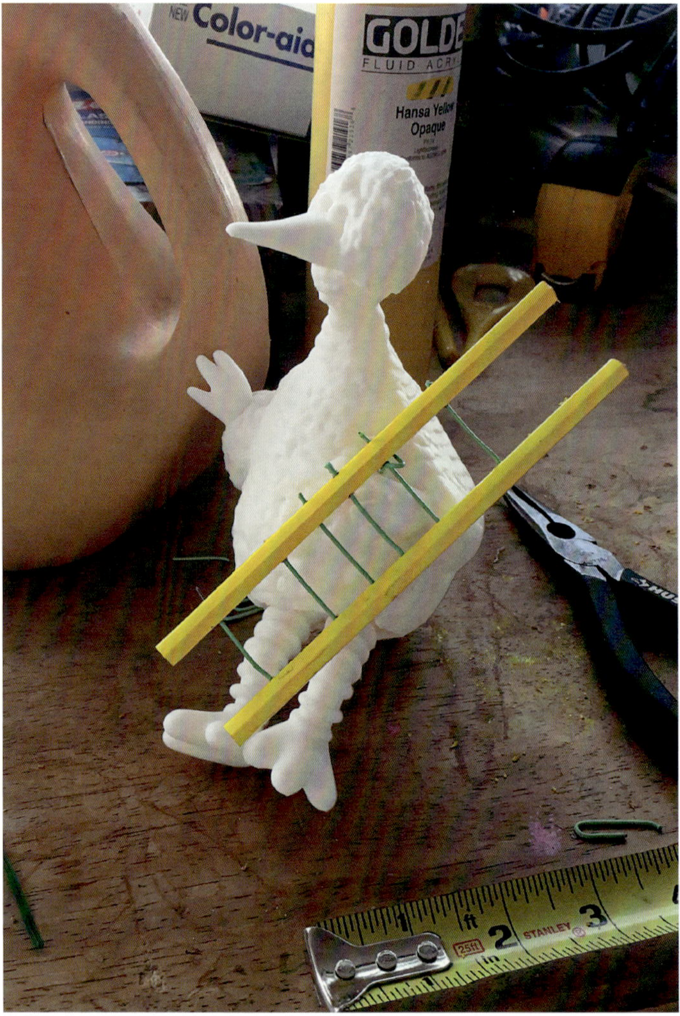

Fig. 19. **Alex Da Corte.** Study for *As Long as the Sun Lasts,* 2021; studio image from 2020

dreams of celestial motion and tidal attraction, of men on moons and women as moons, of celestial light and small steps for mankind, and creates a cliché-proof homage to the earth-ladder-moon. The absurdity of the gesture—of setting the oversized, flightless bird upon the delicate crescent moon, and balancing the character and the ladder on one side of a Calder-like standing mobile—offers the viewer a mirror for the age of collapse. At this moment when monuments have fallen, museums stand exposed, "great" men have been knocked off their plinths, and the fantasies of genius, merit, and egalitarian access have waned, Da Corte picks through the rubble and finds a big bird here, a children's frame there, and pieces together not a new world but an homage to the end of this one. What goes up, the ladder in the frame reminds us, must come down. But between the two motions, Da Corte finds a delicate balance, a pause, an interval, a foot poised above a rung, a *Sesame Street* Muppet swinging on the moon.

Let Da Corte's blue Big Bird represent the necessity of aesthetic surplus, the luxurious indulgence of wasteful performances, the inverse of balance and order, the potential for absurd utopian fantasy. His anti-monumental homage to finality, *As Long as the Sun Lasts,* places the moon, *Sesame Street* Muppets, and humans in new orbits; shakes free of clichéd gestures; and reminds us that balance is just a momentary stability between rising and falling. We all fall down.

Transfiguration: A Conversation with Alex Da Corte

Sheena Wagstaff

Sheena Wagstaff It's been a while since we've talked. You've sent me lots of images of storefronts and a few of ladders since then.

Alex Da Corte I know. What a crazy moment to be doing this talk!

SW It is! But there has to be meaning to this time. Alex, perhaps we should start with Pennsylvania, the state of Warhol, and Heinz ketchup. You've settled in Philadelphia. I want to understand your sense of place, including the fact that Warhol seems to have an importance in your work.

ADC Right after I got out of high school, I wanted to be an animator for Disney. When I went to the School of Visual Arts in New York in 1999–2001, I was on a strict path to do animation and only animation. I somehow remained quite oblivious to contemporary art. I don't even know if I knew who Warhol was until I got to New York. When I realized that painting maybe wasn't what I wanted to do but didn't have the words to describe what it was that I wanted to do, I fell into printmaking. My mind has always been interested in systems-based logic. When I was introduced to printmaking and shown artists that worked in systematic ways like Warhol or Lichtenstein (figs. 20, 21), I just immediately gravitated toward them. At the time, I had been making a lot of work about Heinz ketchup. This idea of making portraits of food or foodstuff was my way into that world and into Warhol. Having grown up near Camden, New Jersey, which is the home of Campbell's Soup, I felt like this kind of art was something I could aspire to, or that it was something I was interested in. In regard to place, I navigate the world in a way that I let coincidence guide me. I find a lot of joy in mining things that are familiar to me. Thinking of my work in relation to my family or in relation to where I stand matters. I dig where I stand. That's urgent to me. I never wanted to be an artist that's colonizing a place. I realized, having moved around quite a bit, that when I am on solid ground, I feel I need to get to know it in order to understand myself.

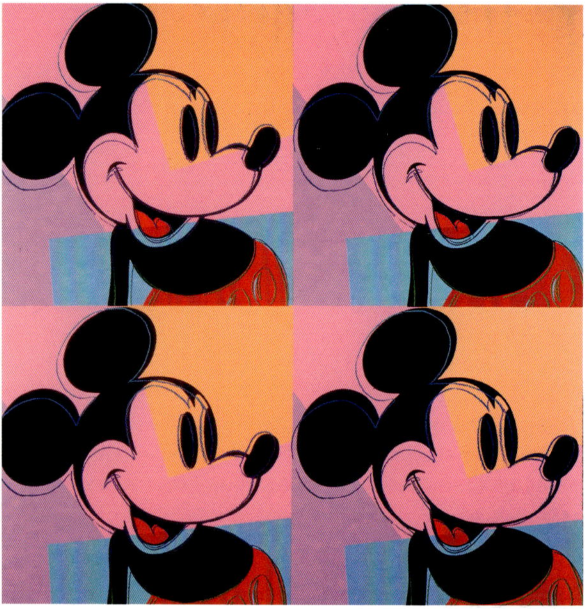

Fig. 20. **Andy Warhol** (American, 1928–1987). *Quadrant Mickey Mouse*, 1981. Synthetic polymer and silk-screen inks on canvas, 60 × 60 in. (152.4 × 152.4 cm)

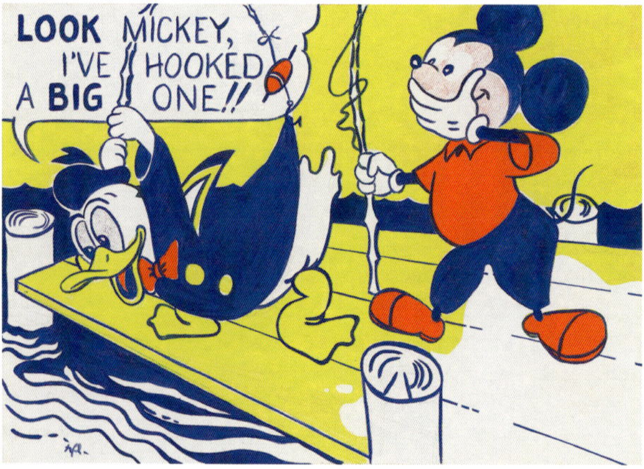

Fig. 21. **Roy Lichtenstein** (American, 1923–1997). *Look Mickey*, 1961. Oil on canvas, 48 × 69 in. (121.9 × 175.3 cm). National Gallery of Art, Washington, D.C., Gift of Roy and Dorothy Lichtenstein in Honor of the 50th Anniversary of the National Gallery of Art (1990.41.1)

SW There does seem to be a deep "Americanness" about your work, notwithstanding the fact that you're half-Venezuelan. Your references to popular imagery—whether they be Life cereal (fig. 22), ketchup, Burger King (fig. 23), or wonderful design from the fifties inspired by film from that era—are endemic to American culture, originating in a time before your era. But you have been very clear that your work is not about nostalgia. Where does this interest come from?

ADC Many years ago, I started an ongoing body of work in relation to Arthur Rimbaud's poem *A Season in Hell* (fig. 24). The poem is about a character who is in this new place, Hell, and is open to what they see. They are looking with big eyes at these new experiences and not rating them or saying they are bad or good. So this idea that one can approach something as cooked as Hell and make it rich or sexy or desirable again was interesting to me. Thinking about my father, who was this alien that came to the States, I wanted to see this world and these things that were common foodstuffs here in the States as if I were him, as if he had arrived in this new place, call it Hell, call it the United States of America. There was a heightened sense of looking, and that looking wouldn't stop. My hunger to see and to learn and to engage and to listen is apparent. For me, the Americanness about it is thinking about how you mine what is here, how you appreciate and look more at what is familiar.

SW Except that you make it unfamiliar, too.

ADC Certainly. I just think that we get into these patterns where we stop looking or we take things for granted.

SW I don't think there is any danger of your being in that position.

ADC So much of my research comes from something as simple as driving to the studio every day. I try to change the pattern of my course so that I might see a backyard that has a garden hose in it that's a certain color or the way that two people are standing on the street talking. For me, it's just saying, "Here are these things that I'm passing every day." I can learn from that. They don't have to be in the epicenter of some world where things are provided for me. I have to seek out what it is I care about and try to learn from that.

SW The sense of place is geographical, yet you're also talking about a sense of space and time, which links Warhol and

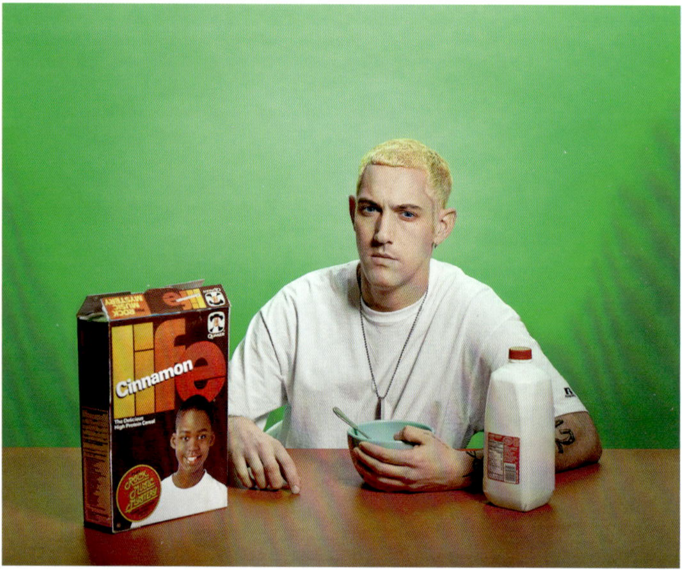

Fig. 22. **Alex Da Corte.** *TRUƎ LIFƎ*, 2013. Archival pigment print, anodized metal frame, 30 × 37 1/2 in. (76.2 × 95.3 cm), 2 A.P., edition of 5

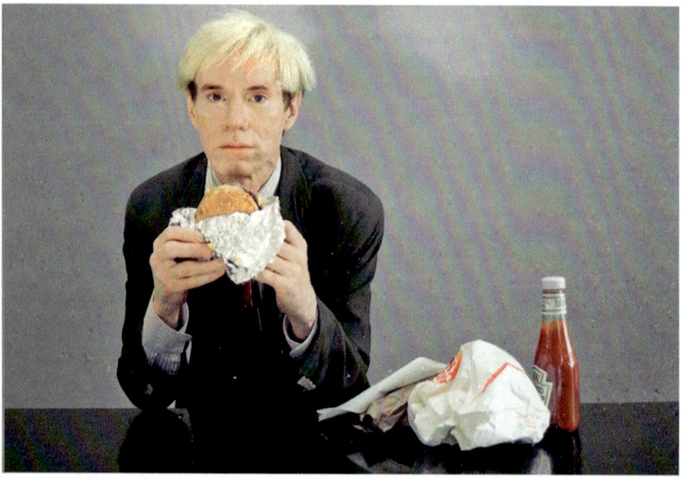

Fig. 23. *Andy Warhol Eating a Hamburger*, 1982. Scene by **Jørgen Leth** (Danish, born 1937) and **Andy Warhol** (American, 1928–1987), originally shown in *66 Scenes from America*

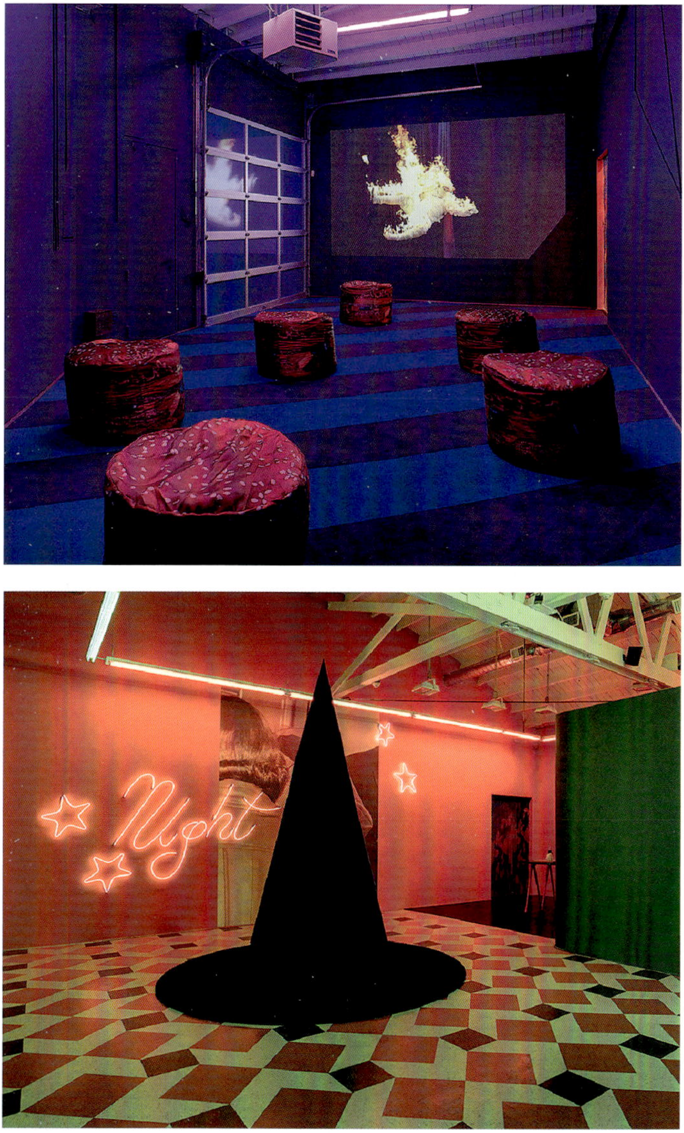

Fig. 24. **Alex Da Corte.** *A Season in He'll,* 2016. Installation views, Art + Practice at the Hammer Museum, Los Angeles

Lichtenstein to the fundamental idea of the comic-strip frame. They create a pared-down, essential image that encapsulates a moment in a narrative. There are so many great early twentieth-century American comic strips, like Winsor McCay's *Little Nemo in Slumberland* and George Herriman's *Krazy Kat* (fig. 25). They were radical pioneers at that time, breaking apart the frame, erupting through the screen—even Walt Disney's *Steamboat Willie*. Were you ever tempted to engage with the self-reflexive aspect of animation?

ADC Absolutely—it was like a fetish that I developed. From very early on, my only access to these things was animation books that I found in stores. They weren't books you could find in the local library; they were books like Frank Thomas and Ollie Johnston's *The Illusion of Life*, and John Canemaker's *Dreams in Motion*, and Bob Thomas's *Art of Animation*. In a self-reflexive way, I wanted to be a Disney animator because I wanted to participate in a community of people who made worlds that transported me, that saved me. But I think in reality I wouldn't have been a good animator.

SW Except that you have done exactly what you said that cartoons did for you: you said they "made worlds that transported me." That is what you do in your installations or your videos. You don't need to draw them in order to create those worlds.

ADC Right, I realize that I became an animator of inanimate things. I give life to things that are rote or are ruins in some ways or are just detritus of a past time. I reanimate them, so maybe I am a reanimator. Although I didn't understand it as performance then, the extension of the line of experiencing your body and whatever is in front of you is animation. You're thinking about it before, and you're thinking about what's to come. I guess when I say "systems-based logic," I am constantly just tying together loose ends to say, *These incongruent things can become congruent or not, but you can learn from whatever it is that collides when they come together*. I always think of my family, about these two worlds that combined but maybe shouldn't, or didn't know each other. My mother, who is American, was born in New Jersey with Welsh and German ancestry, and then my father is Venezuelan. They were from different worlds, two different classes, two different ethos. They were married and became some kind of unit of incongruency. That is what my work is trying to do. It's about trying to marry materials that maybe would never speak to each other and trying to reconcile what that difference is.

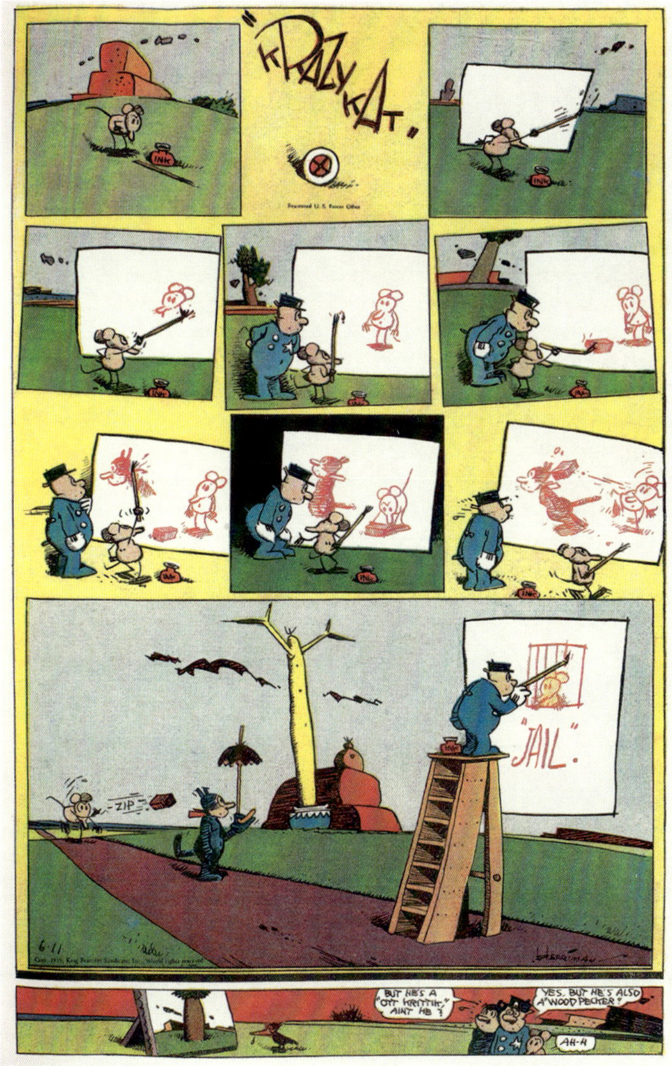

Fig. 25. **George Herriman** (American, 1880–1944). *Krazy Kat*, June 11, 1939

SW You use images that have multiple sources of inspiration. In an interview in your *True Life* book (2020), you talked about Warhol as a Christlike figure. In some earlier moment in your career you also talked about the meaning of ketchup and its color: the red of blood, the redness of the devil in *Rubber Pencil Devil*, red as a carrier of the symbolism of passion. Warhol was a devout practitioner of Catholicism, which is a religion full of symbolism. He went regularly to Mass, a fact that was only discovered after his death. One can see aspects of religion lying at the base of much of his work. And I see this in your work too. I'm not trying to essentialize it to a specific aspect of interpretation, but there is a transformational, transcendent aspect to your work: the way you use liquid, your creation of a parallel belief system. You create things with their own internal logic. Do you feel that that is true? Is it something you're actively working with—or against?

ADC I think I could be with and against. I don't know if I ever told you, but for a long while I thought I would be a priest.

SW No, you didn't.

ADC In my early twenties, St. Augustine's *Confessions* and St. Louis de Montfort's writings were really important to me. I was very devout to St. John Neumann, and really felt a strong relationship to Our Lady and to, of course, Our Lady of Fátima. For political and personal reasons, I moved away from those things, but I never really lost the love of allegory and storytelling through symbols. I was very close to my mother's father. He was a very poor man, who was a devout Catholic and really glorified Michelangelo's work. I had a poster of *The Last Judgment* hanging on my wall, and we would talk about it as the highest form of art: the stories that were embedded in *The Last Judgment*, the flayed skin of St. Bartholomew (fig. 26), the dubious pope who was painted as a demon in the bottom right. These stories were integral to how I understood that art was a way of storytelling. The flayed skin was both a self-portrait of Michelangelo and a way of depicting the oppressions he felt from the church at the time. These things became essential to the way I view an image. For me, when I first started making things, it was important that I could bring my family along: they are devout Catholics. As I grew away from the church, I was like, "But I'm not growing away. I can just be a bridge to something else. I can still make work that speaks to your beliefs and upholds your love for 'X,' and then also speaks to that difference or speaks to what it takes to bridge that gap." There is oil and water in me.

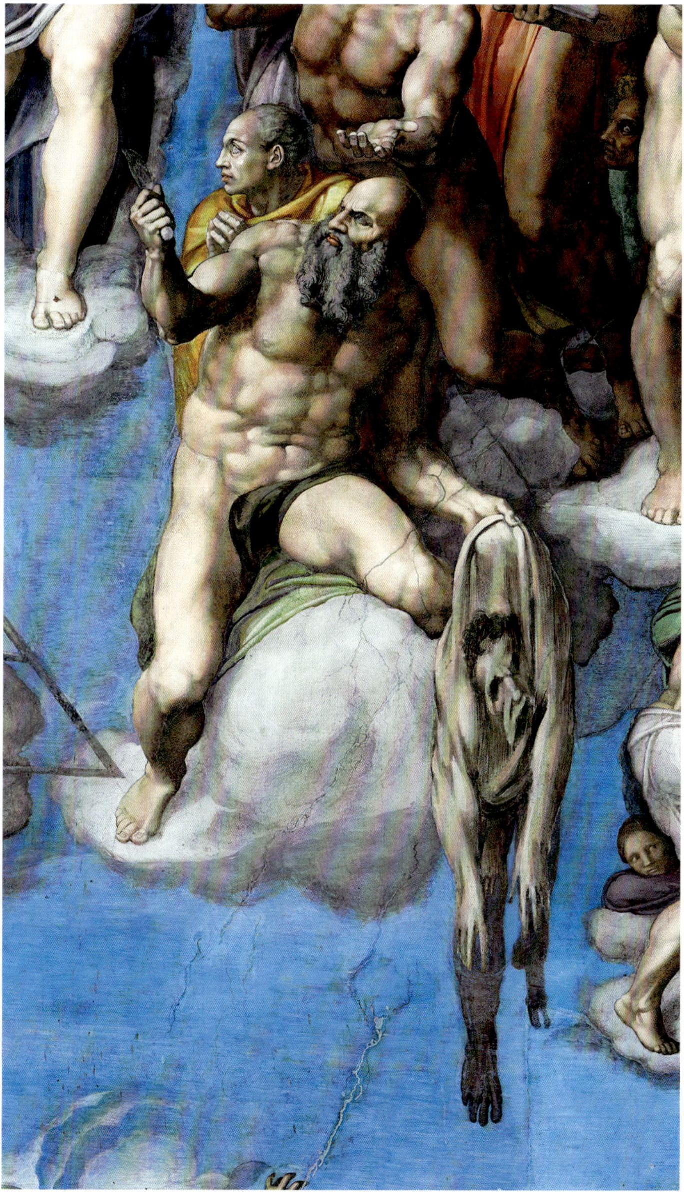

Fig. 26. **Michelangelo Buonarroti** (Italian, 1475–1564). St. Bartholomew and the flayed skin, detail of *The Last Judgment*, 1534–41. Fresco. Sistine Chapel, Vatican City

There is this constant polarity that's very much indebted to the Spirit and alchemy. It tugs at my heart when you say that, because it's a very complicated thing for me—my relationship to the Spirit. I put it in my work.

SW Thank you for sharing that, Alex.

ADC No one has ever asked me that before. My relationship to my internal and external realities being at war with each other is quite important to my work. I remember being in New York with a group of artists who had different politics or thoughts on religion or weren't religious. It seemed easy to collect together in a safe city and be accepted. I always thought that although I could be much freer that way, I never wanted to abandon my family. Although they were different than me, I wanted to bring them along. I wanted to spend my life bridging that gap; not that it's a harder road or that I'm some victim in this, but I just thought this is a way to move forward, to actually confront that difference.

SW I want to return to St. Bartholomew being skinned alive: from one point of view, it seems absurd that one can kill someone by peeling his surface off. But pain is inherent in the work; we are drawn to empathize with the extraordinary suffering he undergoes. I am interested in what you were saying about skin, about your taking on the persona of another: in your performances, you morph into so many different types of people and beings.

ADC I remember always thinking about how the skin that you live in can defy you, that even your own skin, which we think we know so well, can be deceiving. My work became thinking about how to look and see and understand the Other. I first made a relationship to that kind of looking with John Carpenter's film *Halloween* and the character Michael Myers (fig. 27); here is this villainous figure looking into a home at an idyllic family and trying to understand them but not understanding them at all. In him I saw a figure I wanted to empathize with. I wanted to try to rewrite the script on how that person was navigating the world to say, "Maybe they weren't villainous, but they were just trying to understand their family better by looking at them inside their home."

SW The power of empathy: how far is one able to enter the mindset of another, especially in such an extreme way? Some of the greatest filmmakers are those who create stories from a different point of view. Pedro Almodóvar, whom I associate with your work, tells complex stories. It isn't until later in the movie one understands the dark side to the lighthearted, visually luscious story. Many of his films have these gorgeous, saturated colors that you use in your work: highly stylized and choreographed, with a controlled scenography. In this case, it's a different kind of skin. You are creating something that is a kind of parallel universe, but it is of the world nonetheless.

ADC I've always been drawn to Almodóvar's films. *All About My Mother* was one of the earliest films of his I saw (fig. 29). In it, no character, no position of power, is ever really fixed, and it features a very complicated dialogue that reflects a rambunctious, combative relationship to oneself and to the one that one loves or one wants to be. The navigation between all of this difference still appeals to me. I always think about the person that you are versus the person that you want to be.

SW Who do you want to be?

ADC I always feel like I could do better.

SW Each one of your works is a combination of many different inspirations. I recognize some of them, while others are new. What impresses me is that you are able to reduce an image to a potent, essential form. How do you reach that point of selection? Do you lie awake at night, sifting through options?

ADC There's a lot of lying awake at night. None of these images or ideas need me in their life, but I want to understand them. These images say so much, so it's a question of how you undo this legibility, and say, "No, actually this is much more complicated." We have to insist on new ways of looking at familiar things and the stories that they have to tell. We haven't asked enough questions of ourselves as participants. I recently made a painting called *The Future Is on Fire or: Grenade in My Mouth or . . .* (2020, fig. 30) that is inspired by a comic book cover in which a witch and a little devil are looking at a crystal ball, and it's on fire. This led me to think about how Puff the Magic Dragon might see that same flame as their own disembodied flame, outside their body in this crystal ball. I imagined a story of a dragon considering their inside spirit and saying, "Maybe it's not found yet, but it's somewhere in the future." It was this idea of heroism or aspiration or wanting something of your life.

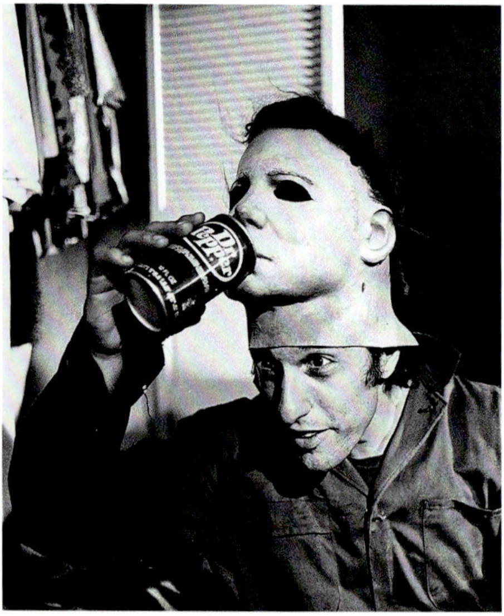

Fig. 27. Actor Nick Castle as Michael Myers on the set of *Halloween*, 1978, directed by **John Carpenter** (American, born 1948)

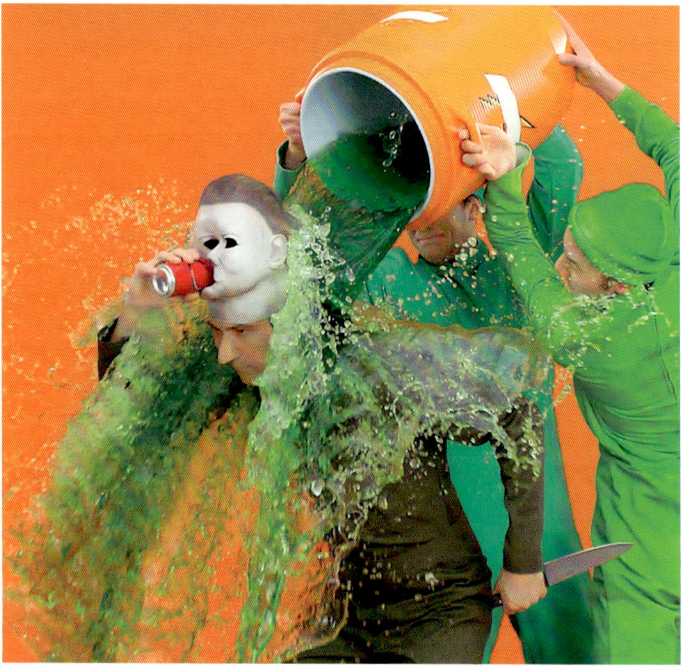

Fig. 28. **Alex Da Corte.** *Rubber Pencil Devil*, 2018. Video, color, sound, 159 min., 22 sec.

SW Another aspect of your work to which so many people respond is your identifiable design aesthetic. You have a remarkable sense of design and color. There's something extraordinary about the way that you bring disparate colors together. You violate the rules of complementary colors; you disrupt them.

ADC Color is huge; it's everything to me. When we see color reproduced in the world of things, we must remember this is evidence of invisible labor. These color selections have real urgency, and we have to reconcile them, even if those selections are meant to entertain or sell, even if the sweet or the savory or the saccharine color of plastic is meant to indulge. There's something there to deconstruct and understand. I see that in something as simple as the color of an M&M. These are things that kind of wash over you as a child. It's why I insist on this kind of reevaluation of familiar things. Not to say that everything needs to be reevaluated in order to undo it or deflate it, but there are just many lines of thought embedded in the smallest decisions. Color is always in flux. I think that's something that drives me.

SW Like the yellow bird that becomes the blue bird . . .

ADC Exactly. And how can that be? How can even something that fixed and certain defy you or surprise you? There's this fluidity in life that troubles me; it also brings me joy.

SW I like that, because it gives one hope! Going back, you talked about sentimentality. That's always a risk when you're engaging with images that come freighted with this kind of saccharine power. Even someone like Big Bird comes close. Is that something that concerns you?

ADC Surely. I think that's the challenge in working with these characters, in that it appears as though there is no criticism there. You run the risk of saying, "You're embracing this sweet thing. Who cares? There are people in cages right now." But there's another side to this story; it's just that we're not acknowledging it. To consider lovable things like Calder and Big Bird is not to say that they are without critique. I want to know why they are what they are. What does it say about the land that we stand on, that's raised these things up so high, but still is a land that's so troubled? What is it that we've done? I think this just goes back to this idea that what one person says is lovable is grotesque to another. I guess I just want to make room for all of those voices, for those that are cynical or those that are on the

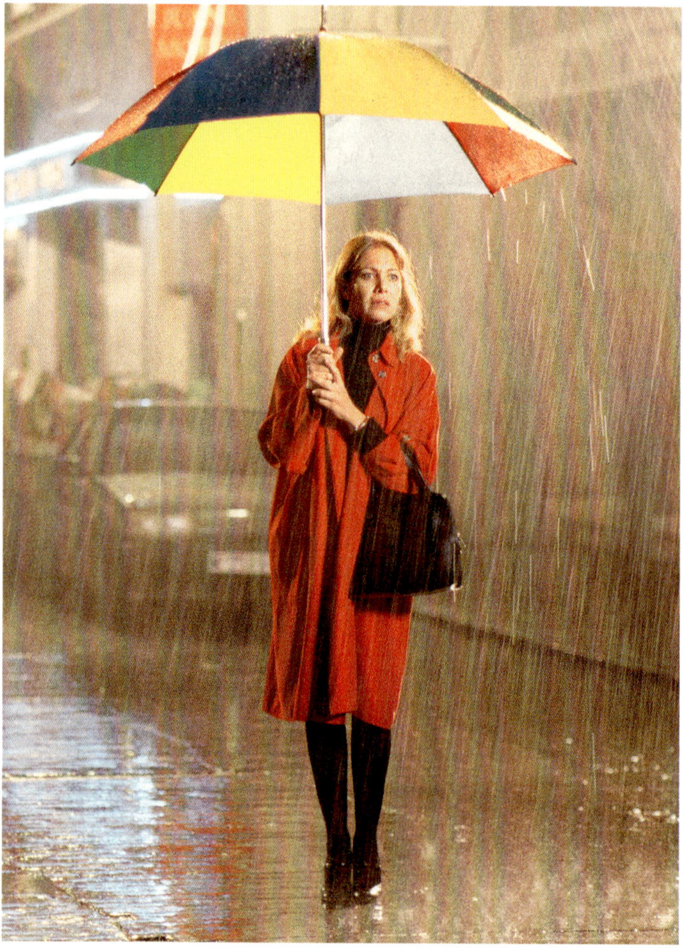

Fig. 29. Still from *All About My Mother* (*Todo sobre mi madre*), 1999, directed by **Pedro Almodóvar** (Spanish, born 1949)

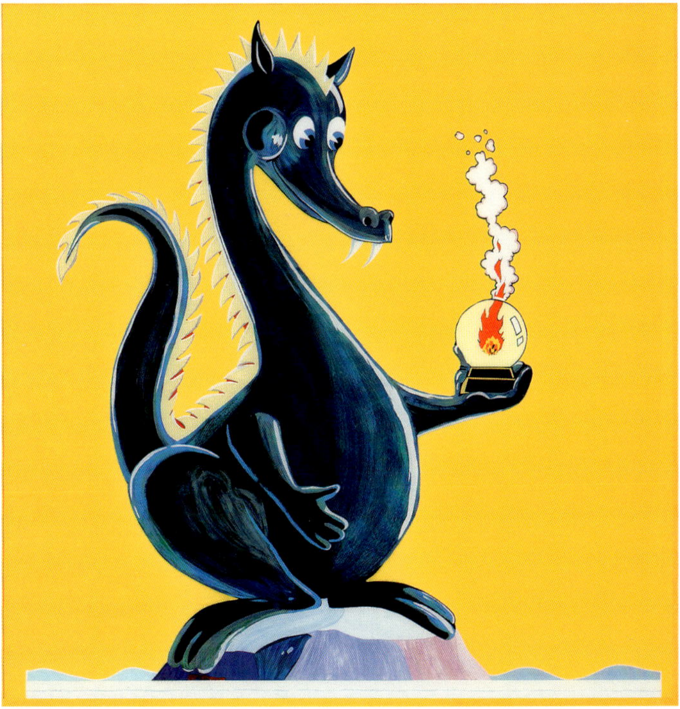

Fig. 30. **Alex Da Corte.** *The Future Is on Fire or: Grenade in My Mouth or . . .* , 2020. Plexiglass, Flashe paint, sequin pins, foam, velvet, hardware, wood frame, 73 1⁄4 × 73 1⁄4 × 3 in. (186 × 186 × 7.5 cm)

periphery that say, "I actually don't want to participate in that way." I'm not getting on the boat with Big Bird and saying, "Happy sails!" I'm wanting to search for the miraculous even with something as benign as Big Bird.

SW I guess I was also thinking about aesthetics. You have deliberately moved beyond that in your work.

ADC I don't want to have any taste. It's something I strive for. I want to be able to change and adapt, because I want to listen more. I want to listen more, and I want to learn more.

As Long as the Sun Lasts, 2021

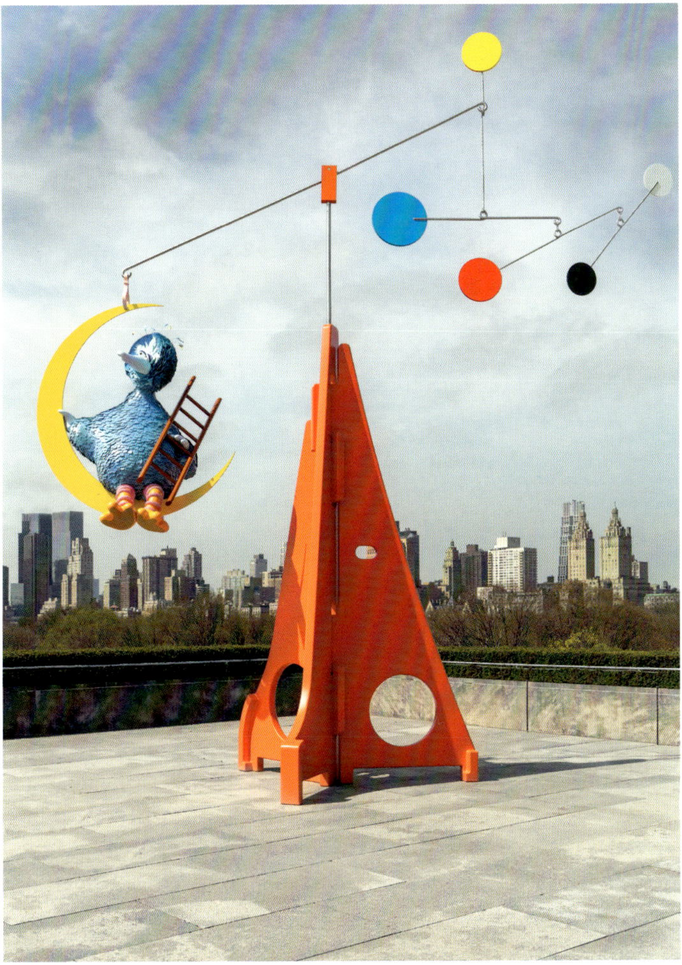

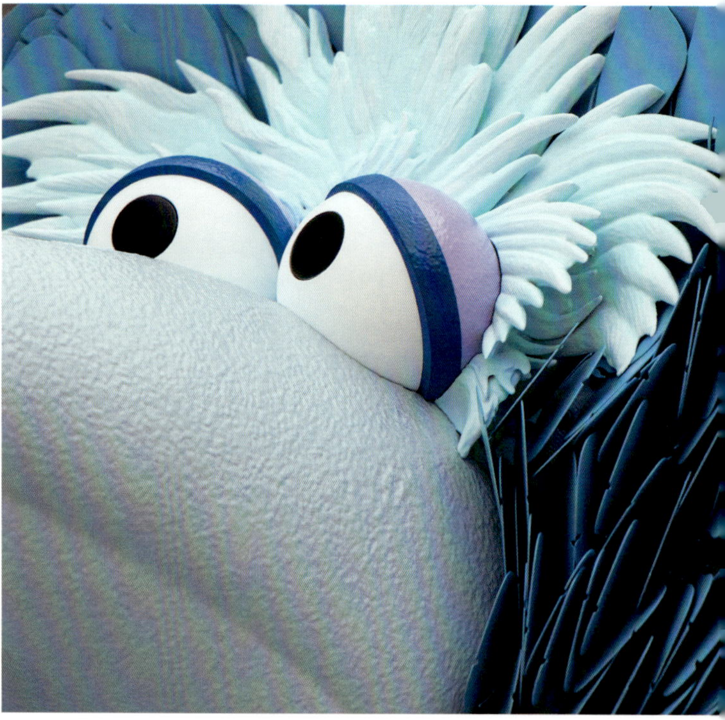
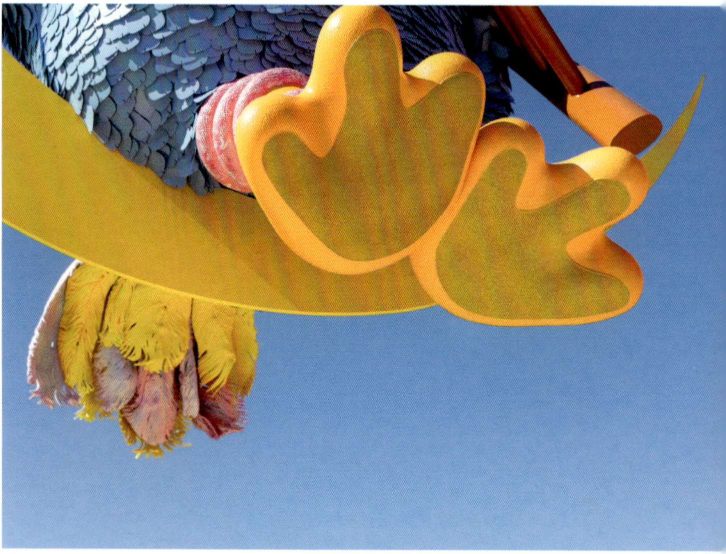

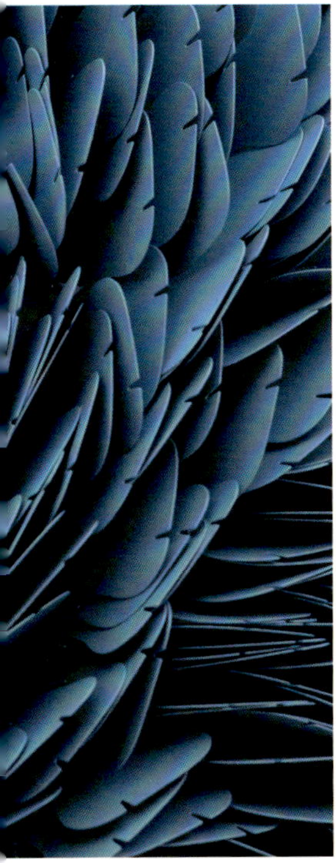

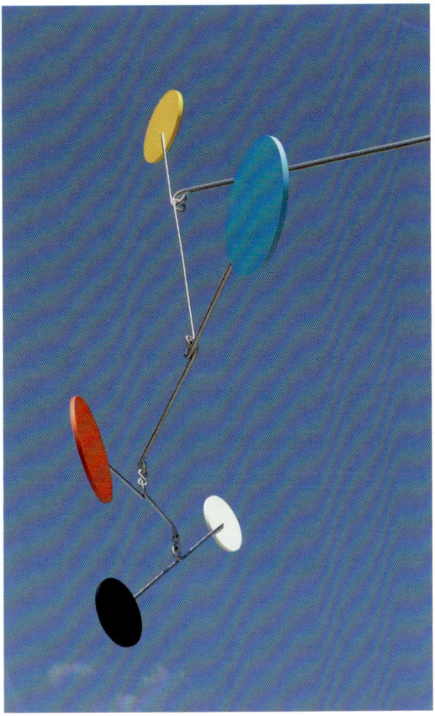

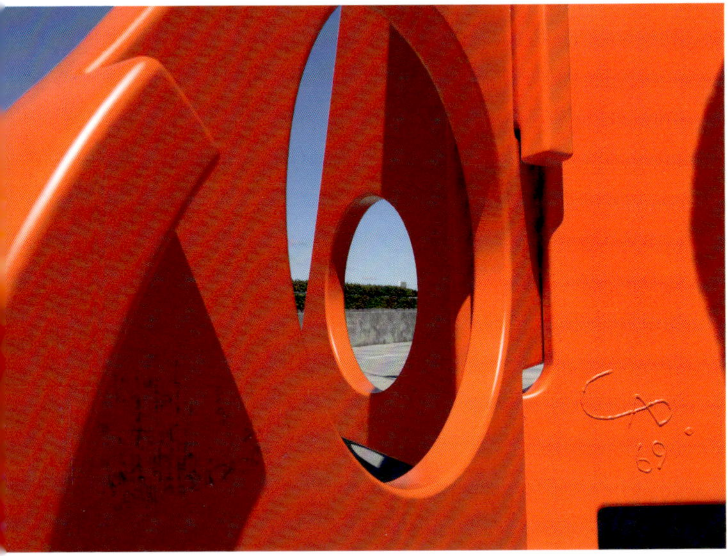

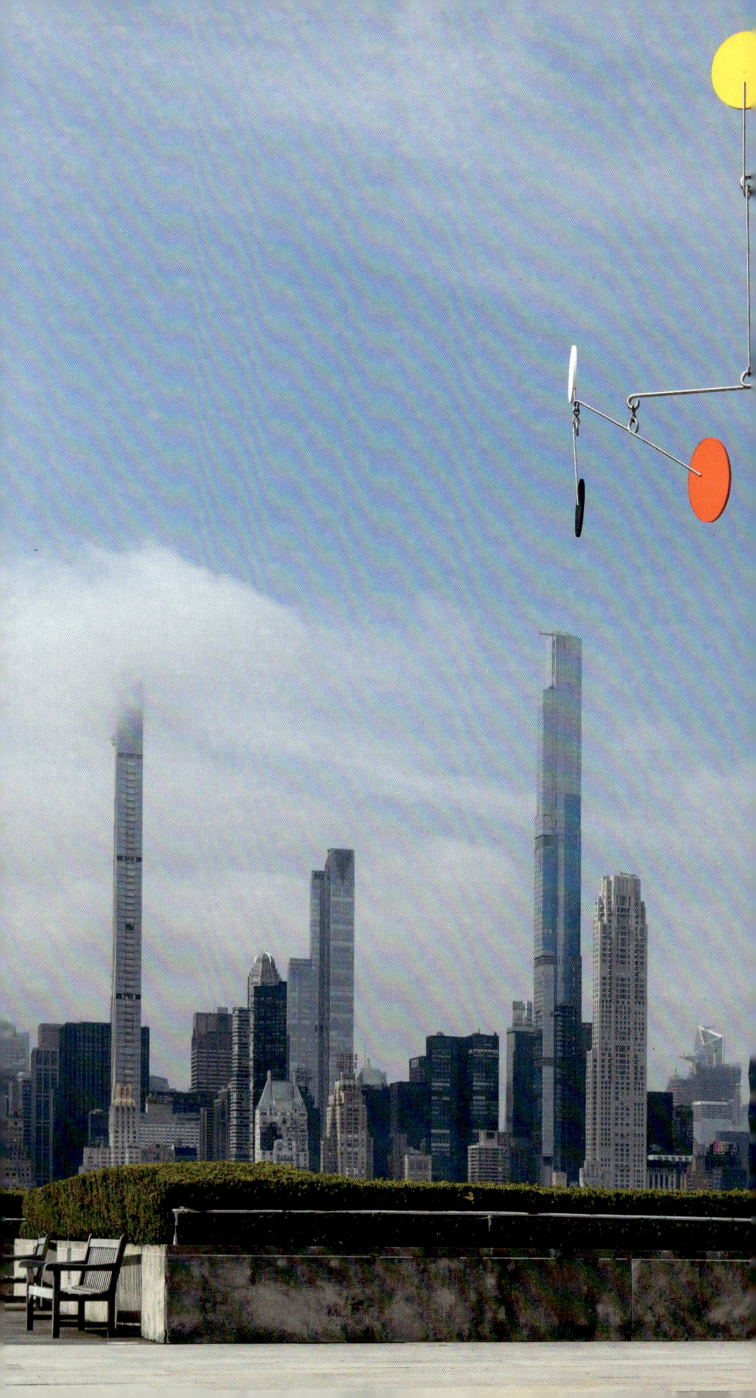

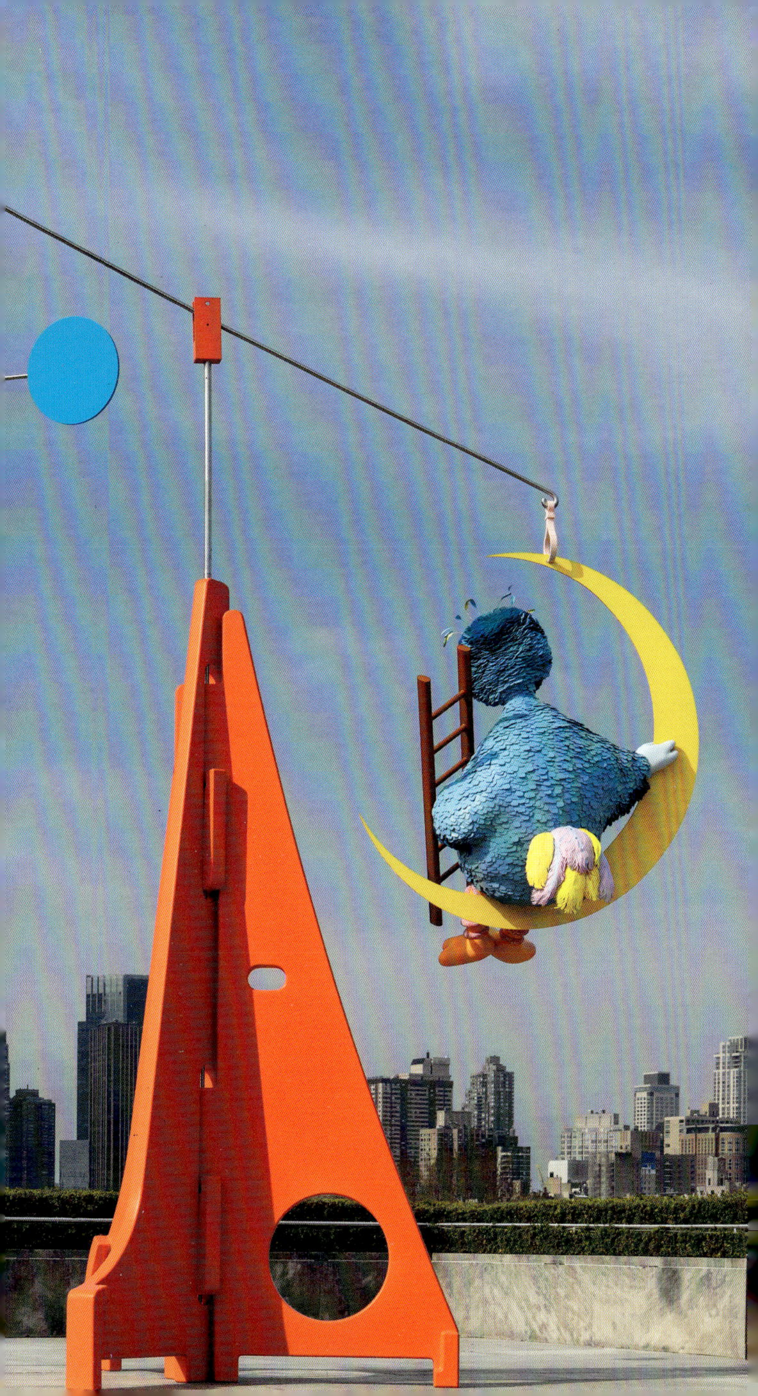

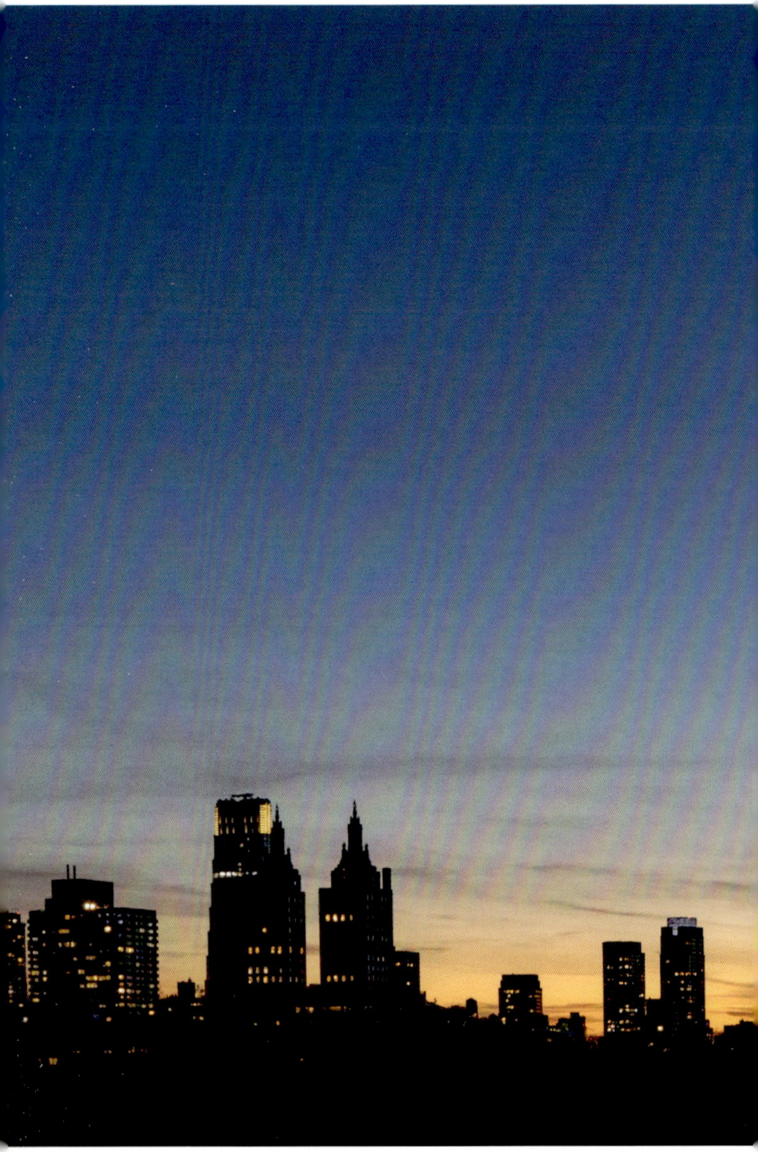

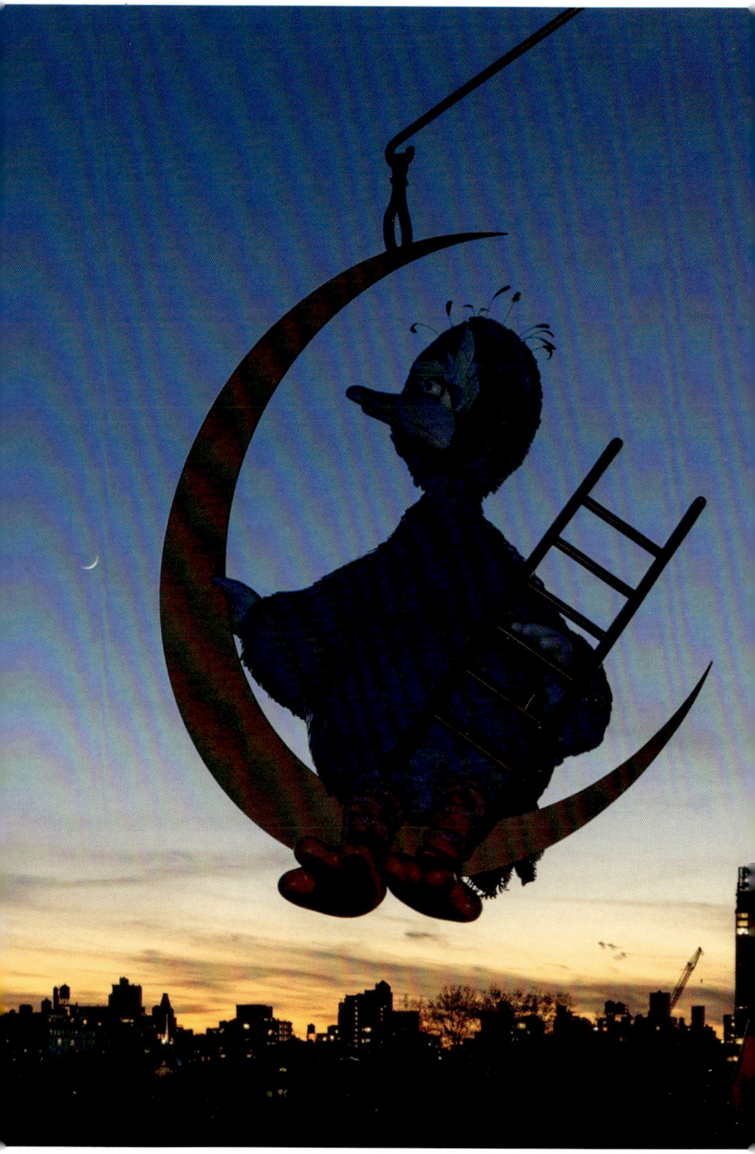

Selected Exhibition History

Solo Exhibitions

2020
Helter Shelter or: The Red Show! or . . ., Sadie Coles HQ, London

Rubber Pencil Devil, Prada Rong Zhai, Shanghai

2018
THƎ SUPƎRMAN, Kölnischer Kunstverein, Cologne

2017
Slow Graffiti, Secession, Vienna

2016
50 Wigs, HEART Herning Museum of Contemporary Art, Denmark

A Season in He'll, Art + Practice at the Hammer Museum, Los Angeles

Free Roses, Massachusetts Museum of Contemporary Art, North Adams

2015
Le Miroir Vivant, Museum Boijmans Van Beuningen, Rotterdam

Die Hexe, Luxembourg & Dayan, New York

2014
Easternsports (with Jayson Musson), Institute of Contemporary Art, University of Pennsylvania, Philadelphia

Delirium I, David Risley Gallery, Copenhagen

2013
Body Without Organs (with Sean FitzGerald), Fjord Gallery, Philadelphia

1 O O O I S L A N D, Joe Sheftel Gallery, New York

As Is Wet Hoagie (with Borna Sammak), Oko, New York

Fun Sponge, Institute of Contemporary Art at Maine College of Art, Portland

Bacon Brest, Artspeak, Vancouver

CAR WHORE, Wake Gallery, Detroit

2012
Candy Rain, Joe Sheftel Gallery, New York

2011
The Island Beautiful/Mortal Mirror [curated by Alex Da Corte], Bodega/Extra Extra Galleries, Philadelphia

2010
The Kind of Dog That Keeps You Waiting, Yale School of Art galleries, New Haven

2009
Activity #91, Golden Age, Chicago

2005
The Death of All Things Beautiful, Window on Broad, Rosenwald-Wolf Gallery, University of the Arts, Philadelphia

Selected Group Exhibitions

2020
Reinvention of Allan Kaprow's *Chicken* (1962), presented in conjunction with *Invisible City: Philadelphia and the Vernacular Avant-Garde*, University of the Arts, Philadelphia

Citizenship: A Practice of Society, Museum of Contemporary Art Denver

For a Dreamer of Houses, Dallas Museum of Art

2019
Ancient History of the Distant Future, Pennsylvania Academy of the Fine Arts, Philadelphia

Garlands, Treignac Projet, France

May You Live in Interesting Times, 58th Venice Biennale

The Other Apartment, The Mattress Factory, Pittsburgh, and Sazmanab, Tehran

2018
Double Takes: Historic and Contemporary Film + Video, Museum of Contemporary Art Cleveland

57th Carnegie International, Carnegie Museum of Art, Pittsburgh

Warhol 1968, Moderna Museet, Stockholm

Strange Attractors: The Anthology of Interplanetary Folk Art, Redling Fine Art, Los Angeles

Collections, Musée d'Art Contemporain de Lyon, France

2016
Dreamlands: Immersive Film and Cinema and Art, 1905–2016, Whitney Museum of American Art, New York

Illumination: New Contemporary Art at Louisiana, Louisiana Museum of Modern Art, Humlebæk, Denmark

Fire under Snow: New Film and Video Works at Louisiana, Louisiana Museum of Modern Art, Humlebæk, Denmark

The 5th of July, Atlanta Contemporary Art Center

2015
La vie moderne, 13th Lyon Biennial

2014
The New Beauty of Our Modern Life, Higher Pictures, New York

2013
Camp Paradox Days, Rosenwald-Wolf Gallery, University of the Arts, Philadelphia

Paint Things: Beyond the Stretcher, deCordova Sculpture Park and Museum, Lincoln, Mass.

2012

First Among Equals, Institute of Contemporary Art, University of Pennsylvania, Philadelphia

2011

Seemed Like a Good Idea at the Time, Platform Gallery, Winnipeg, Canada

That's How We Escaped: Reflections on Warhol, Institute of Contemporary Art, University of Pennsylvania, Philadelphia

ICA Open Video Call 2011/2012, Institute of Contemporary Art, University of Pennsylvania, Philadelphia

SUBstainability: Science, Policy & Opportunity, Texas State University Galleries, San Marcos

2010

New Skin for the Old Ceremony, Hammer Museum, Los Angeles

Cellar Door: Front Room Series, Alex Da Corte, Trevor Reese, and Justin Visnesky, Contemporary Art Museum St. Louis

2009

Between Spaces, MoMA PS1, New York

2008

Love Explosion, Fleisher/Ollman Gallery, Philadelphia

L'Autre, Rosenwald-Wolf Gallery, University of the Arts, Philadelphia

This Is This, Institute of Contemporary Art, University of Pennsylvania, Philadelphia

2005

Turning Pages, Wardman Library, Whittier College, California

Further Reading

Barthes, Roland. *Mythologies*, translated by Annette Lavers. New York: Hill and Wang, 1972.

Borges, Jorge Luis. *Dreamtigers*, translated by Mildred Boyer et al. Austin: University of Texas Press, 1964.

Calvino, Italo. *The Complete Cosmicomics*, translated by Martin McLaughlin, Tim Parks, and William Weaver. London: Penguin Classics, 2009.

Carlin, John, and Sheena Wagstaff. *The Comic Art Show: Cartoons in Painting and Popular Culture*. Exh. cat., Whitney Museum of American Art. New York: Fantagraphics Books, 1983.

Carson, Anne. *Autobiography of Red: A Novel in Verse*. New York: Alfred A. Knopf, 1998.

Cavallo, Adolfo S. *The Unicorn Tapestries in The Metropolitan Museum of Art*. New York: The Metropolitan Museum of Art, 1998.

Cross, Susan, and Alex Da Corte, eds. *Alex Da Corte: Free Roses*. Exh. cat., 2016–17. North Adams, Mass.: Massachusetts Museum of Contemporary Art; Munich: Del Monico Prestel, 2016.

Da Corte, Alex, and Jayson Musson. *Alex Da Corte and Jayson Musson: Easternsports*. Exh. cat., Philadelphia: Institute of Contemporary Art, 2016.

Da Corte, Alex, et al. *Alex Da Corte: True Life*, edited by William Pym. Cologne: Verlag der Buchhandlung Walther und Franz König, 2020.

Finch, Christopher. *Of Muppets & Men: The Making of the Muppet Show*. New York: Muppet Press/Alfred A. Knopf, 1981.

Frank, Hannah. *Frame by Frame: A Materialist Aesthetics of Animated Cartoons*, edited by Daniel Morgan. Oakland, Calif.: University of California Press, 2019.

Goethe, Johann Wolfgang von. *The Sorrows of Young Werther*, translated by Thomas Carlyle and R. D. Boylan. Mineola, N.Y.: Dover Publications, 2002.

Gygax, Raphael, Heike Munder, and Judith Welter, eds. *Toys Redux: An Anthology on Play as Critical Action*, translated by Gerrit Jackson and Christian Quatmann. Exh. cat., Migros Museum für Gegenwartskunst. Zurich: JRP Ringier, 2015.

Hainley, Bruce, Alex Da Corte, and Robert Nickas. *Alex Da Corte: Slow Graffiti*. Exh. cat., Vienna Secession. Berlin: Revolver Publishing, 2017.

Leonardo da Vinci. *The Notebooks of Leonardo da Vinci*, translated by Edward McCurdy. Old Saybrook, Conn.: Konecky & Konecky, 2003.

Lipman, Jean, and Margaret Aspinwall. *Alexander Calder and His Magical Mobiles*. New York: Hudson Hills Press, 1981.

Nelson, Maggie. *Bluets*. Seattle: Wave Books, 2009.

Perl, Jed. *Calder: The Conquest of Time; The Early Years, 1898–1940*. New York: Alfred A. Knopf, 2017.

———. *Calder: The Conquest of Space; The Later Years, 1940–1976*. New York: Alfred A. Knopf, 2020.
Shelley, Mary Wollstonecraft. *Frankenstein, or, The Modern Prometheus*. New York: James Pott & Co., 1901.
Solnit, Rebecca. *A Field Guide to Getting Lost*. New York: Viking, 2005.

Photography Credits

Acknowledgments

As Song as the Sun Lasts was conceived, developed, and installed during the COVID-19 pandemic. In the face of these unforeseen and challenging circumstances, Alex has presented a project that is truly inspiring and comforting. I will always be beholden to him for his gentleness, patience, and warmth that set a tone for the commission and sustained everyone, myself included, during these benumbing times.

My regards to the Alex Da Corte Studio in Philadelphia, and to Mark Rossi and his team at Handmade in Los Angeles for their dedication to this project.

At The Met, this commission would not have been possible without the enthusiasm of Max Hollein, Marina Kellen French Director, and Daniel H. Weiss, President and CEO, and the vision and advocacy of Sheena Wagstaff, Leonard A. Lauder Chairman, Department of Modern and Contemporary Art. An essential interlocutor, Sheena has offered crucial insight that is borne out in the spirited interview with Alex. Furthermore, the success of this commission is due to the tireless efforts of Senior Manager Pari Stave. Her support and advice have been indispensable.

This catalogue is published in conjunction with *The Roof Garden Commission: Alex Da Corte, As Long as the Sun Lasts,* on view at The Metropolitan Museum of Art, New York, from April 16 through October 31, 2021.

The exhibition is supported by

Bloomberg Philanthropies

Additional support is provided by Cynthia Hazen Polsky and Leon B. Polsky.

The catalogue is made possible by the Mary and Louis S. Myers Foundation Endowment Fund.

Published by The Metropolitan Museum of Art, New York

Mark Polizzotti, Publisher and Editor in Chief

Peter Antony, Chief Production Manager

Michael Sittenfeld, Senior Managing Editor

Edited by Kayla Elam

Designed by Gina Rossi

Production by Lauren Knighton

Image acquisitions and permissions by Shannon Cannizzaro

Photographs of works in The Met collection are by the Imaging Department, The Metropolitan Museum of Art, unless otherwise noted.

All artworks by Alex Da Corte © Alex Da Corte, courtesy of the artist and Matthew Marks Gallery, N.Y., and Sadie Coles HQ, London

Additional photography credits appear on page 62.

Typeset in Galaxie Polaris and Chronicle

Printed on Endurance Silk 100lb

Separations by Professional Graphics, Inc., Rockford, Illinois

Printed and bound by Mittera Group Inc., Parsippany, New Jersey

Bound by Bassil Bookbinding Co., Hackensack, New Jersey

Cover and pp. 1, 53–59: *As Long as the Sun Lasts*, 2021. Photography by Anna-Marie Kellen and Hyla Skopitz

Page 2: Alex Da Corte. Photography by James Emmerman Studio

First printing

The Metropolitan Museum of Art
1000 Fifth Avenue
New York, New York 10028
metmuseum.org

Distributed by
Yale University Press,
New Haven and London
yalebooks.com/art
yalebooks.co.uk

Cataloguing-in-Publication Data is available from the Library of Congress.

ISBN 978-1-58839-729-4

The organization of this commission and the attendant complexities of acquiring all necessary permissions during a pandemic have been agilely managed by Quincy Houghton, Deputy Director for Exhibitions, Amy Desmond Lamberti, Associate General Counsel, Cristina Del Valle, Senior Associate General Counsel, Lisa Silverman Meyers, Head of Licensing and Partnerships, Rachel Ferrante, Touring Exhibitions Project Manager, who then passed the baton to Katy Uravitch, Exhibitions Project Manager, Taylor Miller, Buildings Manager for Exhibitions, Matthew Lytle, Assistant Buildings Manager, Exhibitions, Elsie Alonso, Assistant Registrar, and Meryl Cohen, Chief Registrar.

In the Department of Modern and Contemporary Art, Elizabeth Doorly and Padget Sutherland provided invaluable assistance, while Jose Rivero, Deborah Gul Haffner, and Rebecca McGinnis ensured the safety and security of both art and visitor. Also, I am grateful for Kendra Roth's supervision and expertise as an objects conservator. The Museum's Design team of Frank Mondragon, Anna Rieger, Sarah Parke, and Christopher DiPietro has offered a graphics package that is attentive and sensitive to Alex's own sensibilities.

My colleagues in Development, especially Clyde B. Jones III, Jason Herrick, John L. Wielk, and Jessica M. Sewell, receive my sincerest gratitude for all their efforts to secure the sponsorship that enabled this commission to be possible. In External Affairs, Alexandra Kozlakowski and Kenneth Weine have been instrumental in presenting this visionary commission to the public.

This book is the result of a collaboration with members of The Met's Publications and Editorial Department and the artist. I extend my appreciation to Mark Polizzotti for granting me the option to invite a third contributor to the publication. We are especially fortunate to have an energetic, clever, and delicious text by Jack Halberstam. Thoughtful and patient Kayla Elam has been my committed editor on this publication, offering precise and considered feedback on the texts. The book features a smart design by Gina Rossi, and its production was expertly handled by Lauren Knighton. Shannon Cannizzaro tirelessly tracked down the images, and Hyla Skopitz evocatively captured the installation on the roof. Michael Sittenfeld and Peter Antony are also due recognition for their continuing attention to the Roof Garden catalogues.

Finally, my thanks go to Bloomberg Philanthropies for its sponsorship of this commission and to Cynthia Hazen Polsky and Leon B. Polsky for their steadfast support. This beautiful volume is due to the generosity of the Mary and Louis S. Myers Foundation Endowment Fund, for which I am very grateful.

Shanay Jhaveri
Assistant Curator, International Modern and Contemporary Art
Department of Modern and Contemporary Art

The artist would like to thank:
Shanay Jhaveri, Sheena Wagstaff, Jack Halberstam, Ryan Hart, Mark Rossi, Allison Bona and the folks at Handmade, Kim Nguyen, William Pym, Brooke Kauffman, Carolyn Anello, Tim Rusterholz, Thomas Lauria, Jake Lecuyer, Cara Monroe, Hudson Hatfield, Andrew Smith, Libby Rosa, James Emmerman, Izzi Galindo, Emily Schubert, Grant Schofield, Riley Hanson, Caroll Spinney, Kermit Love, Jim Henson, Sesame Workshop, the Calder Foundation, Donna Summer, Brooke Kamin Rapaport, Jessica Anasti, Vince Gallagher, Matthew Marks, Sadie Coles, Pari Stave, and Max Hollein.

For Americo Da Corte, and all wanderers above and below the sea of fog and my family here, there, and everywhere.